Drug Abuse

Drug Abuse

Other books in the Current Controversies series:

Drug Abuse

Roman Espejo, *Book Editor*

Daniel Leone, *President*
Bonnie Szumski, *Publisher*
Scott Barbour, *Managing Editor*

CURRENT CONTROVERSIES

Cover photo: FPG International

Library of Congress Cataloging-in-Publication Data

Drug abuse / Roman Espejo, book editor.
    p. cm. — (Current controversies)
    Includes bibliographical references and index.
    ISBN 0-7377-0852-2 (pbk. : alk. paper)
    ISBN 0-7377-0853-0 (lib. bdg. : alk. paper)
    1. Drug abuse. 2. Drug abuse—Prevention. 3. Drug abuse—Treatment.
4. Drugs—Law and legislation. I. Espejo, Roman, 1977– . II. Series.

HV5801 .D5776   2002
362.29—dc21   2001051286

Contents

Chapter 2: Is Drug Abuse a Growing Problem?

Yes: Drug Abuse Is a Growing Problem

No: Drug Abuse Is Not a Growing Problem

Chapter 3: Are Drug Treatment and Prevention Programs Effective?

Yes: Drug Treatment and Prevention Programs Are Effective

No: Drug Treatment and Prevention Programs Are Not Effective

percent of young adults who have participated in drug education programs have tried drugs. Drug education must be reevaluated in order to give young people realistic advice on drug abuse.

Chapter 4: Should Drug Policies Be Liberalized?

Yes: Drug Policies Should Be Liberalized

No: Drug Policies Should Not Be Liberalized

Foreword

By definition, controversies are "discussions of questions in which opposing opinions clash" (Webster's Twentieth Century Dictionary Unabridged). Few would deny that controversies are a pervasive part of the human condition and exist on virtually every level of human enterprise. Controversies transpire between individuals and among groups, within nations and between nations. Controversies supply the grist necessary for progress by providing challenges and challengers to the status quo. They also create atmospheres where strife and warfare can flourish. A world without controversies would be a peaceful world; but it also would be, by and large, static and prosaic.

The Series' Purpose

The purpose of the Current Controversies series is to explore many of the social, political, and economic controversies dominating the national and international scenes today. Titles selected for inclusion in the series are highly focused and specific. For example, from the larger category of criminal justice, Current Controversies deals with specific topics such as police brutality, gun control, white collar crime, and others. The debates in Current Controversies also are presented in a useful, timeless fashion. Articles and book excerpts included in each title are selected if they contribute valuable, long-range ideas to the overall debate. And wherever possible, current information is enhanced with historical documents and other relevant materials. Thus, while individual titles are current in focus, every effort is made to ensure that they will not become quickly outdated. Books in the Current Controversies series will remain important resources for librarians, teachers, and students for many years.

In addition to keeping the titles focused and specific, great care is taken in the editorial format of each book in the series. Book introductions and chapter prefaces are offered to provide background material for readers. Chapters are organized around several key questions that are answered with diverse opinions representing all points on the political spectrum. Materials in each chapter include opinions in which authors clearly disagree as well as alternative opinions in which authors may agree on a broader issue but disagree on the possible solutions. In this way, the content of each volume in Current Controversies mirrors the mosaic of opinions encountered in society. Readers will quickly realize that there are many viable answers to these complex issues. By questioning each author's conclusions, students and casual readers can begin to develop the critical thinking skills so important to evaluating opinionated material.

Current Controversies is also ideal for controlled research. Each anthology in the series is composed of primary sources taken from a wide gamut of informational categories including periodicals, newspapers, books, United States and foreign government documents, and the publications of private and public organizations. Readers will find factual support for reports, debates, and research papers covering all areas of important issues. In addition, an annotated table of contents, an index, a book and periodical bibliography, and a list of organizations to contact are included in each book to expedite further research.

Perhaps more than ever before in history, people are confronted with diverse and contradictory information. During the Persian Gulf War, for example, the public was not only treated to minute-to-minute coverage of the war, it was also inundated with critiques of the coverage and countless analyses of the factors motivating U.S. involvement. Being able to sort through the plethora of opinions accompanying today's major issues, and to draw one's own conclusions, can be a complicated and frustrating struggle. It is the editors' hope that Current Controversies will help readers with this struggle.

Greenhaven Press anthologies primarily consist of previously published material taken from a variety of sources, including periodicals, books, scholarly journals, newspapers, government documents, and position papers from private and public organizations. These original sources are often edited for length and to ensure their accessibility for a young adult audience. The anthology editors also change the original titles of these works in order to clearly present the main thesis of each viewpoint and to explicitly indicate the opinion presented in the viewpoint. These alterations are made in consideration of both the reading and comprehension levels of a young adult audience. Every effort is made to ensure that Greenhaven Press accurately reflects the original intent of the authors included in this anthology.

"The argument that drug abuse is a public health issue, rather than a criminal activity, has renewed the debate over existing drug policies."

Introduction

The goal of reducing drug abuse has shaped some of the U.S. government's most uncompromising policies. From the strict surveillance of the U.S.-Mexican border to national antidrug advertising campaigns, federal efforts to reduce drug abuse have relentlessly targeted the supply and demand of illicit drugs. Many of these tactics, including the harsh punishment of drug dealers and habitual drug users, are punitive in nature.

However, the argument that drug abuse is a public health issue, rather than a criminal activity, has renewed the debate over existing drug policies. For instance, the theory that drug addiction is a neurological disorder, not a moral flaw, has caused some to view addicts less as criminals and more as sick individuals who need treatment and compassion. To this end, voters in Arizona and California recently approved measures that give minor drug offenders the choice between rehabilitation and prison. Also, "harm reduction," an approach that focuses not on preventing drug abuse, but instead on reducing the risks associated with drug use, is gaining attention as an alternative to America's hard line drug policies.

Advocates of harm reduction assert that a practical and nonjudgmental approach in confronting drug abuse is more effective than disciplinary action. According to drug expert Robert W. Westermeyer, harm reduction is based on three pragmatic central beliefs. The first belief is that "excessive behaviors occur along a continuum"; the moderate use of substances causes less harm than abuse. The second belief is that "changing addictive behavior is a stepwise process, complete abstinence being the final step." He explains that the harm reduction model "embraces" any movement away from the harms of drug use, no matter how small. The third belief, Westermeyer states, is that "sobriety simply isn't for everybody" and that drug abuse is a fact of life for some individuals. He contends that harm reductionists "hope that addicted individuals will ultimately come to eliminate their high risk behavior completely, though it is accepted that the only way to get people moving in the direction of abstinence is to connect with them 'where they're at.'"

The case of writer and former heroin addict Maia Szalavitz exemplifies the goal of the harm reduction approach: If abstinence is not a choice, the risks of using drugs should be minimized. "I was at risk of AIDS," she says, reflecting upon her intravenous drug use during the mid-1980s. A friend advised her to always either use her own needles or clean a shared needle with bleach and water before using it. By following that advice, Szalavitz did not contract HIV or hepatitis B during her years as an addict. She feels that harm reduction saved her life.

The practice of harm reduction began in the Netherlands in the late 1960s, when health experts proposed that decriminalizing the use of marijuana would reduce the use of cocaine and heroin. They believed that removing marijuana from the illicit drug market would lower marijuana users' exposure to the culture of hard drug abuse. Today in the United States, the harm reduction movement consists mainly of two programs. Methadone maintenance, in which doctors prescribe the synthetic drug methadone to hardened heroin addicts as a less harmful substitute for heroin, generates little controversy. On the other hand, needle-exchange programs, which allow addicts to exchange their used needles for clean ones without fear of legal repercussions, are often the center of heated debates. These programs were first mobilized in the 1980s as a response to the epidemic of HIV and hepatitis B infections among intravenous drug users (IDUs), which was caused by the sharing of infected needles.

Many drug abuse professionals claim that encouraging IDUs to trade their used hypodermic needles for new ones lowers their risk of HIV and hepatitis B infection by preventing drug addicts from sharing needles. According to one study, the Scottish cities of Glasgow and Edinburgh, which experienced similar heroin epidemics in the 1980s, demonstrated the importance of the availability of clean needles for IDUs. Edinburgh, which banned the selling of hypodermic needles at the time, experienced an alarming rate of HIV infection among IDUs—approximately 50 percent tested HIV-positive by 1984. Although more addicts used drugs intravenously in Glasgow, needle distribution was not restricted, and less than 1 percent of its IDUs contracted HIV. In a similar claim, Ethan A. Nadelmann, director of the Lindesmith Center, a drug policy research institute, contends that the halting of federal funds for needle-exchange programs during George Bush's presidential term (1988–1992) resulted in ten thousand more cases of HIV infection.

However, opponents argue that needle-exchange programs do not lower drug addicts' risk of HIV or hepatitis B infection. Psychiatrist Sally L. Satel argues, "Most needle-exchange studies have been full of design errors, the most rigorous ones have actually shown an increase in HIV infection." For instance, a 1997 study in Montreal, Canada, concluded that those who took part in needle-exchange programs were two to three times more likely to contract HIV than addicts who did not participate. Others contend that although needle-exchange programs prevent some cases of HIV, they do not minimize the other threats to physical health and personal safety involved in heroin addiction. One University of Pennsylvania study followed 415 IDUs in Philadelphia for four years. Although 28 people died during the study, only 5 died from HIV-related causes. The majority died from other factors related to their high-risk behavior, including overdoses, kidney failure, and homicide. Besides failing to protect drug users' health, challengers believe that supporting needle-exchange programs sends the message that society condones drug abuse. Barry A. McCaffrey, former head of the Office of National Drug Control Policy, insists that such programs should be abandoned because drug addicts should not be given "more effective means to continue their addiction. . . . The problem isn't dirty needles, it's injection of illegal drugs."

Supporters of harm reduction programs contend that minimizing the harms of drug addiction is imperative in directing addicts away from high-risk conduct. They view drug abuse as spanning a spectrum of behaviors and phases, some of which are less dangerous than others. Because abstinence is the final step, harm reductionists support every movement away from addiction and the harm of using drugs. In contrast, critics of harm reduction argue that many of the programs are ineffective at lowering the risks of drug use. Moreover, they claim that the harm reduction philosophy abandons the hope that abstinence can be achieved for every addict and warn that removing the negative legal consequences from drug abuse will fuel addiction. Harm reduction is just one of the topics discussed in *Drug Abuse: Current Controversies*. Throughout this anthology, drug abuse experts, health care professionals, and others attempt to define the causes and effects of drug abuse and debate the effectiveness of drug laws and regulations. In doing so, the authors provide valuable insights into one of society's pressing social problems.

Chapter 1

What Factors Contribute to Drug Abuse?

Chapter Preface

The National Center on Addiction and Substance Abuse boldly claims that "a child who reaches age twenty-one without smoking, abusing alcohol or using drugs is virtually certain never to do so." Many policy makers and drug abuse professionals do not take the center's claim lightly. In antidrug campaigns and programs, children and adolescents are repeatedly advised to resist the influences of peer pressure, popular music, and films, and to abstain from underage drinking, smoking, and marijuana use.

Efforts are especially aimed at keeping young people from using marijuana due to the "gateway theory" belief that using marijuana increases one's likelihood of using harder drugs. A committee of the American Academy of Pediatrics, for example, claims that "adolescents who use marijuana are 104 times more likely to use cocaine compared with peers who never smoked marijuana," and that "marijuana's role as a 'gateway drug' for some teenagers must be considered." Some suggest that marijuana users go on to try other drugs because they grow tolerant of marijuana's effects. According to columnist Phyllis Schlafly, "The 'high' from pot gradually diminishes and pot smokers often take other drugs to get a kick."

However, detractors contend that the gateway theory fails to hold up when drug abuse patterns are examined closely. Professors Lynn Zimmer and John P. Morgan state, "Over time, as any particular drug increases or decreases in popularity, its relationship with marijuana changes. . . . Cocaine became very popular in the early 1980s as marijuana use was declining." Others suggest that drug abuse is linked more strongly to the traits of the abuser than the use of a gateway drug. "We've long known that everyone reacts to drugs differently," says writer Cynthia Cotts, "and that the risk of addiction is predicted by many factors, such as genetic hard-wiring and social status."

These and other issues are debated in the following chapter, which examines the factors that contribute to drug abuse.

Drug Addiction Is a Disease

by Alan I. Leshner

About the author: *Alan I. Leshner, former deputy director of the National Institute of Mental Health, is director of the National Institute on Drug Abuse.*

Dramatic advances over the past two decades in both the neurosciences and the behavioral sciences have revolutionized our understanding of drug abuse and addiction. Scientists have identified neural circuits that subsume the actions of every known drug of abuse, and they have specified common pathways that are affected by almost all such drugs. Researchers have also identified and cloned the major receptors for virtually every abusable drug, as well as the natural ligands for most of those receptors. In addition, they have elaborated many of the biochemical cascades within the cell that follow receptor activation by drugs. Research has also begun to reveal major differences between the brains of addicted and nonaddicted individuals and to indicate some common elements of addiction, regardless of the substance.

That is the good news. The bad news is the dramatic lag between these advances in science and their appreciation by the general public or their application in either practice or public policy settings. There is a wide gap between the scientific facts and public perceptions about drug abuse and addiction. For example, many, perhaps most, people see drug abuse and addiction as social problems, to be handled only with social solutions, particularly through the criminal justice system. On the other hand, science has taught that drug abuse and addiction are as much health problems as they are social problems. The consequence of this gap is a significant delay in gaining control over the drug abuse problem.

Part of the lag and resultant disconnection comes from the normal delay in transferring any scientific knowledge into practice and policy. However, there are other factors unique to the drug abuse arena that compound the problem. One major barrier is the tremendous stigma attached to being a drug user or, worse, an addict. The most beneficent public view of drug addicts is as victims

Reprinted from "Addiction Is a Brain Disease, and It Matters," by Alan I. Leshner, *Science*, October 3, 1997.

of their societal situation. However, the more common view is that drug addicts are weak or bad people, unwilling to lead moral lives and to control their behaviors and gratifications. To the contrary, addiction is actually a chronic, relapsing illness, characterized by compulsive drug seeking and use. The gulf in implications between the "bad person" view and the "chronic illness sufferer" view is tremendous. As just one example, there are many people who believe that addicted individuals do not even deserve treatment. This stigma, and the underlying moralistic tone, is a significant overlay on all decisions that relate to drug use and drug users.

Ingrained Ideologies

Another barrier is that some of the people who work in the fields of drug abuse prevention and addiction treatment also hold ingrained ideologies that, although usually different in origin and form from the ideologies of the general public, can be just as problematic. For example, many drug abuse workers are themselves former drug users who have had successful treatment experiences with a particular treatment method. They therefore may zealously defend a single approach, even in the face of contradictory scientific evidence. In fact, there are many drug abuse treatments that have been shown to be effective through clinical trials.

These difficulties notwithstanding, I believe that we can and must bridge this informational disconnection if we are going to make any real progress in controlling drug abuse and addiction. It is time to replace ideology with science.

At the most general level, research has shown that drug abuse is a dual-edged health issue, as well as a social issue. It affects both the health of the individual and the health of the public. The use of drugs has well-known and severe negative consequences for health, both mental and physical. But drug abuse and addiction also have tremendous implications for the health of the public, because drug use, directly or indirectly, is now a major vector for the transmission of many serious infectious diseases—particularly acquired immunodeficiency syndrome (AIDS), hepatitis, and tuberculosis—as well as violence. Because addiction is such a complex and pervasive health issue, we must include in our overall strategies a committed public health approach, including extensive education and prevention efforts, treatment, and research.

Science is providing the basis for such public health approaches. For example, two large sets of multisite studies have demonstrated the effectiveness of well-delineated outreach strategies in modifying the behaviors of addicted individuals that put them at risk for acquiring the human immunodeficiency virus (HIV), even if they continue to use drugs and do not want to enter treatment. This approach runs counter to the

> *"Science has taught that drug abuse and addiction are as much health problems as they are social problems."*

broadly held view that addicts are so incapacitated by drugs that they are unable to modify any of their behaviors. It also suggests a base for improved strategies for reducing the negative health consequences of injection drug use for the individual and for society.

What Matters in Addiction

Scientific research and clinical experience have taught us much about what really matters in addiction and where we need to concentrate our clinical and policy efforts. However, too often the focus is on the wrong aspects of addiction, and efforts to deal with this difficult issue can be badly misguided.

Any discussion about psychoactive drugs inevitably turns to the question of whether a particular drug is physically or psychologically addicting. In essence, this issue revolves around whether or not dramatic physical withdrawal symptoms occur when an individual stops taking a drug, what is typically called physical dependence by professionals in the field. The assumption that often follows is that the more dramatic the physical withdrawal symptoms, the more serious or dangerous the drug must be.

This thinking is outdated. From both clinical and policy perspectives, it does not matter much what physical withdrawal symptoms, if any, occur. First, even the florid withdrawal symptoms of heroin addiction can now be easily managed with appropriate medication. Second, and more important, many of the most addicting and dangerous drugs do not produce severe

> *"One major barrier [to treating drug abuse] is the tremendous stigma attached to being a drug user or, worse, an addict."*

physical symptoms upon withdrawal. Crack cocaine and methamphetamine are clear examples: Both are highly addicting, but cessation of their use produces few physical withdrawal symptoms, certainly nothing like the physical symptoms accompanying alcohol or heroin withdrawal.

What does matter tremendously is whether or not a drug causes what we now know to be the essence of addiction: compulsive drug seeking and use, even in the face of negative health and social consequences. These are the characteristics that ultimately matter most to the patient and are where treatment efforts should be directed. These behaviors are also the elements responsible for the massive health and social problems that drug addiction brings in its wake.

Addiction Is a Brain Disease

Although each drug that has been studied has some idiosyncratic mechanisms of action, virtually all drugs of abuse have common effects, either directly or indirectly, on a single pathway deep within the brain [the part of the brain that involves emotion and motivation]. . . . Activation of this system appears to be a common element in what keeps drug users taking drugs. This activity is not unique to any one drug; all addictive substances affect this circuit.

Not only does acute drug use modify brain function in critical ways, but prolonged drug use causes pervasive changes in brain function that persist long after the individual stops taking the drug. Significant effects of chronic use have been identified for many drugs at all levels: molecular, cellular, structural, and functional. The addicted brain is distinctly different from the nonaddicted brain, as manifested by changes in brain metabolic activity, receptor availability, gene expression, and responsiveness to environmental cues. Some of these long-lasting brain changes are idiosyncratic to specific drugs, whereas others are common to many different drugs. The common brain effects of addicting substances suggest common brain mechanisms underlying all addictions.

> *"That addiction is tied to changes in brain structure and function is what makes it, fundamentally, a brain disease."*

That addiction is tied to changes in brain structure and function is what makes it, fundamentally, a brain disease. A metaphorical switch in the brain seems to be thrown as a result of prolonged drug use. Initially, drug use is a voluntary behavior, but when that switch is thrown, the individual moves into the state of addiction, characterized by compulsive drug seeking and use.

Understanding that addiction is, at its core, a consequence of fundamental changes in brain function means that a major goal of treatment must be either to reverse or to compensate for those brain changes. These goals can be accomplished through either medications or behavioral treatments [behavioral treatments have been successful in altering brain function in other psychobiological disorders]. Elucidation [clarification] of the biology underlying the metaphorical switch is key to the development of more effective treatments, particularly antiaddiction medications.

The Social Context

Of course, addiction is not that simple. Addiction is not just a brain disease. It is a brain disease for which the social contexts in which it has both developed and is expressed are critically important. The case of the many thousands of returning Vietnam war veterans who were addicted to heroin illustrates this point. In contrast to addicts on the streets of the United States, it was relatively easy to treat the returning veterans' addictions. This success was possible because they had become addicted while in a setting almost totally different from the one to which they had returned. At home in the United States, they were exposed to few of the conditioned environmental cues that had initially been associated with their drug use in Vietnam. Exposure to conditioned cues can be a major factor in causing persistent or recurrent drug cravings and drug use relapses even after successful treatment.

The implications are obvious. If we understand addiction as a prototypical psychobiological illness, with critical biological, behavioral, and social-context components, our treatment strategies must include biological, behavioral, and social-context elements. Not only must the underlying brain disease be treated, but the behavioral and social cue components must also be addressed, just as they are with many other brain diseases, including stroke, schizophrenia, and Alzheimer's disease.

A Chronic, Relapsing Disorder

Addiction is rarely an acute illness. For most people, it is a chronic, relapsing disorder. Total abstinence for the rest of one's life is a relatively rare outcome from a single treatment episode. Relapses are more the norm. Thus, addiction must be approached more like other chronic illnesses—such as diabetes and chronic hypertension—than like an acute illness, such as a bacterial infection or a broken bone. This requirement has tremendous implications for how we evaluate treatment effectiveness and treatment outcomes. Viewing addiction as a chronic, relapsing disorder means that a good treatment outcome, and the most reasonable expectation, is a significant decrease in drug use and long periods of abstinence, with only occasional relapses. That makes a reasonable standard for treatment success—as is the case for other chronic illnesses—the management of the illness, not a cure.

Addiction as a chronic, relapsing disease of the brain is a totally new concept for much of the general public, for many policymakers, and, sadly, for many health care professionals. Many of the implications have been discussed above, but there are others.

At the policy level, understanding the importance of drug use and addiction for both the health of individuals and the health of the public affects many of our overall public health strategies. An accurate understanding of the nature of drug abuse and addiction should also affect our criminal justice strategies. For example, if we know that criminals are drug addicted, it is no longer reasonable to simply incarcerate them. If they have a brain disease, imprisoning them without treatment is futile. If they are left untreated, their recidivism rates to both crime and drug use are frighteningly high; however, if addicted criminals are treated while in prison, both types of recidivism can be reduced dramatically. It is therefore counterproductive to not treat addicts while they are in prison.

> *"Not only must the underlying brain disease [of drug addiction] be treated, but the behavioral and social cue components must also be addressed."*

At an even more general level, understanding addiction as a brain disease also affects how society approaches and deals with addicted individuals. We need to face the fact that even if the condition initially comes about because of a voluntary behavior (drug use), an addict's brain is different from a nonaddict's brain, and the addicted individual must be dealt with as if he or she is in a different brain state. We have learned to deal with people in different brain states for schizophrenia and Alzheimer's disease. Recall that as recently as the beginning of this century we were still putting individuals with schizophrenia in prisonlike asylums, whereas now we know they require medical treatments. We now need to see the addict as someone whose mind (read: brain) has been altered fundamentally by drugs. Treatment is required to deal with the altered brain function and the concomitant behavioral and social functioning components of the illness.

Understanding addiction as a brain disease explains in part why historic policy strategies focusing solely on the social or criminal justice aspects of drug use and addiction have been unsuccessful. They are missing at least half of the issue. If the brain is the core of the problem, attending to the brain needs to be a core part of the solution.

Drug Addiction Is Not a Disease

by Sally L. Satel

About the author: *Sally L. Satel is a psychiatrist and lecturer in psychiatry at Yale University School of Medicine.*

On November 20, 1995, more than one hundred substance-abuse experts gathered in Chantilly, Virginia for a meeting organized by the government's top research agency on drug abuse. One topic for discussion was whether the agency, the National Institute on Drug Abuse (NIDA), which is part of the National Institutes of Health, should declare drug addiction a disease of the brain. Overwhelmingly, the assembled academics, public-health workers, and state officials declared that it should.

At the time, the answer was a controversial one, but, in the three years since, the notion of addiction as a brain disease has become widely accepted, thanks to a full-blown public education campaign by NIDA. Waged in editorial board rooms, town-hall gatherings, Capitol Hill briefings and hearings, the campaign reached its climax in 1998 when media personality Bill Moyers catapulted the brain-disease concept into millions of living rooms with a five-part PBS special called "Moyers on Addiction: Close to Home." Using imaging technology, Moyers showed viewers eye-catching pictures of addicts' brains. The cocaine-damaged parts of the brain were "lit up"—an "image of desire" was how one of the researchers on Moyers' special described it.

These dramatic visuals lend scientific credibility to NIDA's position. But politicians . . . should resist this medicalized portrait. First, it reduces a complex human activity to a slice of damaged brain tissue. Second, and more importantly, it vastly underplays the paradoxically voluntary nature of addictive behavior. As a colleague said: "We could examine brains all day and by whatever sophisticated means we want, but we would never label someone a drug addict unless he acted like one."

Excerpted from "The Fallacies of No-Fault Addiction," by Sally L. Satel, *Public Interest*, No. 134, pp. 52–67, Winter 1999. Copyright © 1999 by National Affairs, Inc. Reprinted with permission from the author.

No-Fault Addiction

The idea of a "no-fault" disease did not originate at NIDA. For the last decade or so it was vigorously promoted by mental-health advocates working to transform the public's understanding of severe mental illness. Diseases like schizophrenia and manic depressive illness, they properly said, were products of a defective brain, not bad parenting. Until the early 1980s, when accumulated neuroscientific discoveries showed, irrefutably, that schizophrenia was marked by measurable abnormalities of brain structure and function, remnants of the psychiatric profession and much of the public were still inclined to blame parents for their children's mental illness.

NIDA borrowed the brain-disease notion from the modern mental-health movement, understandably hoping to reap similar benefits—greater acceptance of its efforts and of its own constituent sufferers, that is, addicts. By focusing exclusively on the brain, NIDA ironically diminishes the importance of its own research portfolio, which devotes an ample section to behavioral interventions. It may well be that researchers will someday be able to map the changes in brain physiology that accompany behavioral changes during recovery. Nevertheless, it is crucial to recognize that the human substrate upon which behavioral treatments work, first and foremost, is the will.

Some of those experts that met in Chantilly would say that emphasizing the role of will, or choice, is just an excuse to criminalize addiction. Clinical experience in treating ad-

> *"We could examine brains all day . . . but we would never label someone a drug addict unless he acted like one."*

dicts, however, suggests that such an orientation provides therapeutic grounds for optimism. It means that the addict is capable of self-control—a much more encouraging conclusion than one could ever draw from a brain-bound, involuntary model of addiction.

What Does Brain Disease Mean?

A recent article in the journal *Science*, "Addiction Is a Brain Disease, and It Matters," authored by NIDA director Alan I. Leshner, summarizes the evidence that long-term exposure to drugs produces addiction: Taking drugs elicits changes in neurons in the central nervous system that compel the individual to take drugs. Because these changes are presumed to be irreversible, the addict is perpetually at risk for relapse.

> Virtually all drugs of abuse have common effects, either directly or indirectly, on a single pathway deep within the brain. . . . Activation of this pathway appears to be a common element in what keeps drug users taking drugs. . . . The addicted brain is distinctly different from the non-addicted brain, as manifested by changes in metabolic activity, receptor availability, gene expression and responsiveness to environmental cues. . . . That addiction is tied to

changes in brain structure and function is what makes it, fundamentally, a brain disease.

Others are less dogmatic. Harvard biochemist Bertha Madras acknowledges a virtual library of documented, replicable brain changes with drug exposure, but she also points out that there have been no scientific studies correlating them with behavior.

> *"The addict is capable of self-control—a much more encouraging conclusion than one could ever draw from a brain-bound, involuntary model of addiction."*

Not even Alcoholics Anonymous, the institution most responsible for popularizing the disease concept of addiction, supports the idea that drug-induced brain changes determine an addict's behavior. AA employs disease as a metaphor for loss of control. And even though AA assumes that inability to stop drinking, once started, is biologically driven, it does not allow this to overshadow AA's central belief that addiction is a symptom of a spiritual defect, and can thus be overcome through the practice of honesty, humility, and acceptance.

The brain-disease advocates, of course, operate by an entirely different frame of reference. To them, "addiction" means taking drugs compulsively because the brain, having already been changed by drugs, orders the user to do so. As Moyers put it on "Meet the Press," drugs "hijack the brain . . . relapse is normal." The brain-disease advocates assume a correlation between drug-taking behavior and brain-scan appearance, though one has yet to be clearly demonstrated, and speculate, based on preliminary evidence, that pathological changes persist for years. A physiological diagnosis, to stretch the meaning of that word, should of course yield a medicinal prescription. So, brain-disease advocates seem confident, despite evidence to the contrary, that a neuroscience of addiction will give rise to pharmaceutical remedies. Meanwhile, the search for a cocaine medication, having begun with such high hopes, has come up empty. And there is good reason to wonder if this enterprise will ever bear fruit. Even the widely used medication for heroin addiction—methadone—is only partly helpful in curtailing drug use. It fails to remedy the underlying anguish for which drugs like heroin and cocaine are the desperate remedy.

Addicted to Politics

The dispute over whether addiction is a brain disease isn't merely a dispute among doctors. It is, for many reasons, political. The efforts of NIDA do not simply aim to medicalize addiction, presumably a medical concern, but to destigmatize the addict, clearly a sociopolitical concern. This is also the agenda of the newly formed group, Physician Leadership on National Drug Policy. "Concerted efforts to eliminate stigma" should result in substance abuse being "accorded parity with other chronic, relapsing conditions insofar as access to care, treatment benefits and clinical outcomes are concerned," a statement from the Leadership group says. These sentiments have been echoed by the Institute of Medicine, a quasi-governmental body that is part of the National Academy of Sciences. "Addiction . . . is not well understood by the public and policy makers. Overcoming problems of stigma and misunderstanding will require educating the public, health educators, policymakers and clinicians, highlighting progress made, and recruiting talented researchers into the field."

Indeed, the politics of drug addiction have begun to strain the logic of drug-addiction experts. In their *Lancet* article, "Myths About the Treatment of Addiction," researchers Charles O'Brien and Thomas McLellan state that relapse to drugs is an inherent aspect of addiction and should not be viewed as a treatment failure. They sensibly point out that in long-term conditions—for example, asthma, diabetes, and hypertension—relapse is often the result of the patient's poor compliance with proper diet, exercise, and medication. But then they jump to the conclusion that since the relapse of some addicts follows from poor compliance too, addiction is like any other disease. This is incorrect. Asthmatics and diabetics who resist doctor's orders share certain characteristics with addicts. But asthmatics and diabetics can also deteriorate spontaneously on the basis of unprovoked, unavoidable primary, physical reasons alone; relapse to addiction, by contrast, invariably represents a voluntary act in conscious defiance of "doctor's orders." The bottom line is that conditions like asthma and diabetes are not developed through voluntary behavior. An asthmatic does not choose to be short of breath. Addicts, however, choose to use drugs.

Changing the Public Views of Addiction

Analogies aside, calling addiction a chronic and relapsing disease is simply wrong. Treatment-outcome studies do support the claim, but data from the large Epidemiologic Catchment Area (ECA) study, funded by the National Institute of Mental Health, show that in the general population remission from drug dependence (addiction) and drug abuse is the norm. Contra publicist Bill Moyers and researchers O'Brien and McLellan, relapse is not. According to ECA criteria for remission—defined as no symptoms for the year just prior to the interview—59 percent of roughly 1,300 respondents who met lifetime criteria were free of drug problems. The average duration of remission was 2.7 years, and the mean duration of illness was 6.1 years with most cases lasting no more than 8 years.

> *"The politics of drug addiction have begun to strain the logic of drug-addiction experts."*

Yet, if NIDA and other public-health groups can change how the public views addiction, tangible political gains will follow. Such groups aim at securing more treatment and services for addicts, expanded insurance coverage, and increased funding for addiction research. These are not unreasonable aims insofar as substandard quality of care, limited access to care, and understudied research questions remain serious problems. But the knee-jerk reflex to decry stigma has been naively borrowed from the mental-health community. Stigma deters unwanted behaviors, and it enforces societal norms. Destigmatizing addicts (recasting them as chronic illness sufferers) threatens one of the most promising venues for anti-addiction efforts: the criminal justice system. The courts and probation services can impose sanctions that greatly enhance retention and prevent relapse.

A Medical Cure for Addiction?

One of NIDA's major goals has been the development of a cocaine medication by the turn of the century. Now with two years to go, no magic bullet is in sight. To date, over 40 pharmaceuticals have been studied in randomized controlled trials in humans for cocaine abuse or dependence. Some of these were intended to block craving, others to substitute for cocaine itself, but none have yet been found even minimally effective. The NIDA director has downgraded predictions about the curative power of medication, promoting it as potentially "complementary" to behavioral therapy.

The basic problem with putative anticraving medications is their lack of specificity. Instead of deploying a surgical strike on the neuronal site of cocaine yearning, these medications end up blunting motivation in general and may also depress mood. Likewise, experiments with cocaine-like substances have proven frustrating.

"The knee-jerk reflex to decry stigma [of drug abusers] has been naively borrowed from the mental-health community."

Instead of suppressing the urge to use the drug, they tend to work like an appetizer, producing physical sensations and emotional memories reminiscent of cocaine itself, triggering a hunger for it. . . .

Another pharmacological approach to cocaine addiction has been immunization against the drug's effect. In late 1995, scientists reported the promising effects of a cocaine vaccine in rats. The animals were inoculated with an artificial cocaine-like substance that triggered the production of antibodies to cocaine. When actual cocaine was administered, the antibodies attached to the molecules of cocaine, reducing the amount of free drug available in the bloodstream to enter the brain.

The vaccine is still being developed for use in humans, but the principle behind its presumed effect is already being exploited by an available anti-heroin medication called naltrexone. Naltrexone blocks opiate molecules at the site of attachment to receptors on the neuron. This way, an addict who administers heroin feels no effect. . . . Though naltrexone is effective, most heroin addicts reject it in favor of methadone's calming effect.

Optimism surrounding the pharmaceutical approach to drug dependence stems, in fact, from the qualified success of methadone, an opioid painkiller developed by German chemists during World War II. . . .

Unlike heroin, which needs to be administered every four to eight hours to prevent withdrawal symptoms, methadone requires only daily dosing. "Successful methadone users are invisible," the director of the Beth Israel Medical Center in New York City told the *New York Times*. Between 5 percent and 20 percent remain on the medication for over 10 years, and many are indeed invisible. An example mentioned in the *Times* article is Jimmie Maxwell, an 80-year-old jazz trumpet player who has stayed clean for the past 32 years by taking methadone every day. Unfortunately, people like Maxwell, who lead an optimal life and are otherwise drug-free, represent perhaps 5 percent to 7 percent of methadone patients. Moreover, patients in methadone maintenance are frequently not drug-free; as many as 35 percent to 60 percent also use cocaine or other illicit drugs or black-market sedatives. During a six-year follow-up, D. Dwayne Simpson of the Institute of Behavioral Research at Texas Christian University found over half of all patients were readmitted to their agency at some point.

> *"The course of addictive behavior can be influenced by the very consequences of the drug-taking itself."*

This should come as little surprise. Methadone will only prevent withdrawal symptoms and the related physiological hunger for heroin, but it alone can't medicate the psychic deficits that led to addiction, such as deep-seated inabilities to tolerate boredom, depression, stress, anger, loneliness. The addict who initiated heavy drug use in his teens hasn't even completed the maturational tasks of adolescence, let alone prepared himself psychologically to solve the secondary layer of troubles that accumulated over years of drug use: family problems, educational deficiencies, disease, personal and economic losses. Only a fraction of heroin addicts become fully productive on methadone alone.

The biological view of addiction conceals an established fact of enormous and pressing clinical relevance: The course of addictive behavior can be influenced by the very consequences of the drug-taking itself. Indeed, when the addict reacts to aversive sequelae of drug use—economic, health, legal, and personal—by eventually quitting drugs, reducing use, changing his pattern of use or getting help, he does so voluntarily. Rather than being the inevitable, involuntary product of a diseased brain, the course addiction follows may represent the essence of a free will. Consequences can inspire a change in voluntary behavior, irrespective of its predictability or biological underpinnings. Involuntary behavior cannot be changed by its consequences. A review of the clinical features of addiction will help illustrate the mix of voluntary and involuntary behaviors associated with addiction, belying the claim that addiction is a brain disease. . . .

A regular user in the midst of a cocaine binge or experiencing heroin withdrawal cannot readily stop using if drugs are available. He is presumably in the "brain-disease" state, when use is most compulsive, neuronal disruption most intense. True, even purposeful behavior can occur in this state—for example, the attempt, sometimes violent, to get money or drugs is highly goal-directed. But, at the same time, addicts in such an urgent state will ignore their screaming babies, frantically gouge themselves with dirty needles, and ruin families, careers, and reputations.

Nonetheless, most addicts have broken the cycle many times. Either they decide to go "cold turkey" or end up doing so, unintentionally, by running out of drugs or money or landing in jail. Some heroin addicts admit themselves to the hospital to detoxify because they want to quit, others to reduce the cost of their habit, knowing they'll be more sensitive to the effects of heroin afterward. This latter trip to the hospital, while motivated by an effort to pursue drug use more efficiently, is nonetheless a purposeful move that, under other circumstances, might be taken by the addict to re-exert control.

In the days between binges, cocaine addicts make many deliberate choices including (potentially) the choice to stop using. Heroin-dependent individuals, by comparison, use the drug several times a day but can be quite functional in all respects as long as they have stable access to some form of opiate drug in order to prevent withdrawal symptoms. . . .

The temporal architecture of an addict's routine reveals periods in which the individual is capable of reflection and deliberate behavior. During the course of a heroin addict's day, for example, he may feel rather calm, and his thoughts might be quite

> *"Most addicts . . . decide to go 'cold turkey' or end up doing so, unintentionally, by running out of drugs or money or landing in jail."*

lucid, if he is confident of access to drugs and if he is using it in doses adequate to prevent withdrawal symptoms, but not large enough to sedate. Likewise, there are periods within a cocaine addict's week when he is neither engaged in a binge nor wracked with intense craving for the drug. During such moments, does anyone believe the addict is the victim of a brain disease? . . .

Taking Control

Labeling addiction a chronic and relapsing brain disease is mere propaganda. By downplaying the volitional dimension of addiction, the brain-disease model detracts from the great promise of strategies and therapies that rely on sanctions and rewards to shape self-control. And by reinforcing a dichotomy between punitive and clinical approaches to addiction, the brain-disease model devalues the enormous contribution of criminal justice to combating addiction. The fact that many, perhaps most, addicts are in control of their actions and appetites for circumscribed periods of time shows that they are not perpetually helpless victims of chronic disease. They are the instigators of their own addiction, just as they can be the agents of their own recovery.

Marijuana Is a Gateway Drug

by Joseph A. Califano Jr.

About the author: *Joseph A. Califano Jr. is president of the National Center on Addiction and Substance Abuse. He served as secretary of health, education, and welfare reform from 1977 to 1979.*

"FEDS GO TO POT" screamed the *New York Post* headline in March 1999, after the Institute of Medicine (IOM) released its report "Marijuana and Medicine: Assessing the Science Base." The Associated Press (AP) reported that the IOM had found "there was no conclusive evidence that marijuana use leads to harder drugs."

Misleading Accounts

A look at the actual report shows that these press accounts are misleading. Consider these words from the report: "Not surprisingly, most users of other illicit drugs have used marijuana first. In fact, most drug users begin with alcohol and nicotine before marijuana—usually before they are of legal age. In the sense that marijuana use typically precedes rather than follows initiation of other illicit drug use, it is indeed a 'gateway' drug. But because underage smoking and alcohol use typically precede marijuana use, marijuana is not the most common, and is rarely the first, 'gateway' to illicit drug use."

Those are the words that precede the tentatively worded statement the AP paraphrased: "There is no conclusive evidence that the drug effects of marijuana are causally linked to the subsequent abuse of other illicit drugs." The report notes, however, that "people who enjoy the effects of marijuana are, logically, more likely to be willing to try other mind-altering drugs than are people who are not willing to try marijuana or who dislike its effects. In other words, many of the factors associated with a willingness to use marijuana are, presumably, the same as those associated with a willingness to use other illicit drugs." And the report recognizes "intensity" of marijuana use as increasing the risk of progression to other drugs.

The medical benefits and risks of marijuana—the subjects to which the report devotes most of its attention—are matters for doctors, scientists and the Food and Drug Administration. The potential of marijuana as a gateway drug is a matter of concern for teenagers, parents and policy makers. The IOM's brief, three-page discussion of the gateway issue fails to discuss mounting statistical and scientific evidence that children who smoke pot are much likelier than those who don't to use drugs like cocaine, heroin and LSD. And the press coverage has been dangerously deceptive. The Institute of Medicine study fails to discuss mounting scientific evidence that children who smoke pot are much likelier to use drugs like cocaine, heroin and LSD.

> *"The potential of marijuana as a gateway drug is a matter of concern for teenagers, parents and policy makers."*

I have not read or heard in any news report the important finding that "the . . . interpretation . . . that marijuana serves as a gateway to the world of illegal drugs in which youths have greater opportunity and are under greater social pressure to try other illegal drugs . . . is the interpretation most often used in the scientific literature, and is supported by—although not proven by—the available data."

Potent Correlations

The National Center on Addiction and Substance Abuse (CASA), which I head, analyzed the data from the Centers for Disease Control and Prevention's 1995 Youth Risk Behavior Survey of 11,000 ninth through 12th graders, adjusting for other risk factors such as repeated acts of violence and sexual promiscuity.

The correlations are potent:

- Teens who drank and smoked cigarettes at least once in the past month are 30 times more likely to smoke marijuana than those who didn't.
- Teens who drank, smoked cigarettes, and used marijuana at least once in the past month are more than 16 times as likely to use another drug like cocaine, heroin or LSD.

To appreciate the significance of these relationships, consider this: The first Surgeon General's report on smoking and health found a nine to 10 times greater risk of lung cancer among smokers. The early returns from the monumental Framingham heart study found that individuals with high cholesterol were two to four times as likely to suffer heart disease.

Most people who smoke pot do not move on to other drugs, but then only 5% to 7% of cigarette smokers get lung cancer. The point for parents and teens is that those youngsters who smoke pot are at vastly greater risk of moving on to harder drugs. CASA's studies reveal that the younger and more often a teen smokes pot, the more likely that teen is to use cocaine. A child who uses marijuana before age 12 is 42 times more likely to use cocaine, heroin or other drugs than one who first smokes pot after age 16.

The IOM report also fails to discuss findings of recent scientific studies that suggest some of the reasons for this high correlation. Studies in Italy reveal that marijuana affects levels of dopamine (the substance that gives pleasure) in the brain in a manner similar to heroin. Gaetana DiChiara, the physician who led this work at the University of Cagliari, indicates that marijuana may prime the brain to seek substances that act in a similar way. Studies in the U.S. have found that nicotine, cocaine and alcohol also affect dopamine levels.

Nor does the IOM report mention studies at the distinguished Scripps Research Institute in California and Cumplutense University in Madrid which found that rats subjected to immediate cannabis withdrawal exhibited changes in behavior similar to those seen after withdrawal of alcohol, cocaine and opiates. *Science* magazine called this "the first neurological basis for a marijuana withdrawal syndrome, and one with a strong emotional component shared by other drugs." Alan Leshner, director of the National Institute on Drug Abuse, has estimated that at least 100,000 individuals are in treatment because of marijuana use. Most are believed to be teenagers.

Send Teens a Clear Message

Our concern should be to prevent teen drug use. We know that someone who gets to age 21 without smoking, using drugs or abusing alcohol is virtually certain never to do so. We have known for some time, as the IOM report confirms, that marijuana harms short-term memory, motor skills and the ability to concentrate, attributes teenagers need when they are learning in school.

Parents, teachers and clergy need to send teens a clear message: Stay away from pot. The incompleteness of the IOM report and the press's sloppy summaries of it must not be permitted to dilute that message.

Marijuana Use Does Not Lead to Harder Drugs

by the Institute of Medicine

About the author: *The Institute of Medicine (IOM), associated with the National Academy of Sciences, is a private organization that aims to improve health and science policies on the federal, public, and private levels.*

Millions of Americans have tried marijuana, but most are not regular users. In 1996, 68.6 million people—32% of the U.S. population over 12 years old—had tried marijuana or hashish at least once in their lifetime, but only 5% were current users. Marijuana use is most prevalent among 18- to 25-year-olds and declines sharply after the age of 34. Whites are more likely than blacks to use marijuana in adolescence, although the difference decreases by adulthood.

Most people who have used marijuana did so first during adolescence. Social influences, such as peer pressure and prevalence of use by peers, are highly predictive of initiation into marijuana use. Initiation is not, of course, synonymous with continued or regular use. A cohort of 456 students who experimented with marijuana during their high school years were surveyed about their reasons for initiating, continuing, and stopping their marijuana use. Students who began as heavy users were excluded from the analysis. Those who did not become regular marijuana users cited two types of reasons for discontinuing. The first was related to health and well-being; that is, they felt that marijuana was bad for their health or for their family and work relationships. The second type was based on age-related changes in circumstances, including increased responsibility and decreased regular contact with other marijuana users. Among high school students who quit, parental disapproval was a stronger influence than peer disapproval in discontinuing marijuana use. In the initiation of marijuana use, the reverse was true. The reasons cited by those who continued to use marijuana were to "get in a better mood or feel better." Social factors were not a significant predictor of continued use. Data on young adults show similar trends. Those who use drugs in response to social influences are more likely to stop using them than those who also use them for psychological reasons. . . .

Many factors influence the likelihood that a particular person will become a drug abuser or an addict; the user, the environment, and the drug are all important factors. The first two categories apply to potential abuse of any substance; that is, people who are vulnerable to drug abuse for individual reasons and who find themselves in an environment that encourages drug abuse are initially likely to abuse the most readily available drug—regardless of its unique set of effects on the brain.

The third category includes drug-specific effects that influence the abuse liability of a particular drug. . . . The more strongly reinforcing a drug is, the more likely that it will be abused. The abuse liability of a drug is enhanced by how quickly its effects are felt, and this is determined by how the drug is delivered. In general, the effects of drugs that are inhaled or injected are felt within minutes, and the effects of drugs that are ingested take a half hour or more. . . .

Progression of Drug Use

The fear that marijuana use might cause, as opposed to merely precede, the use of drugs that are more harmful is of great concern. To judge from comments submitted to the Institute of Medicine (IOM) study team, it appears to be of greater concern than the harms directly related to marijuana itself. The discussion that marijuana is a "gateway" drug implicitly recognizes that other illicit drugs might inflict greater damage to health or social relations than marijuana. Although the scientific literature generally discusses drug use progression between a variety of drug classes, including alcohol and tobacco, the public discussion has focused on marijuana as a "gateway" drug that leads to abuse of more harmful illicit drugs, such as cocaine and heroin.

There are strikingly regular patterns in the progression of drug use from adolescence to adulthood. Because it is the most widely used illicit drug, marijuana is predictably the first illicit drug that most people encounter. Not surprisingly, most users of other illicit drugs used marijuana first. In fact, most drug users do not begin their drug use with marijuana—they begin with alcohol and nicotine, usually when they are too young to do so legally.

The Stepping Stone Hypothesis vs. the Gateway Theory

The gateway analogy evokes two ideas that are often confused. The first, more often referred to as the "stepping stone" hypothesis, is the idea that progression from marijuana to other drugs arises from pharmacological properties of marijuana itself. The second is that marijuana serves as a gateway to the world of illegal drugs in which youths have greater opportunity and are under greater social pressure to try other illegal drugs. The latter interpretation is most often used in the scientific literature, and it is supported, although not proven, by the available data.

The stepping stone hypothesis applies to marijuana only in the broadest sense. People who enjoy the effects of marijuana are, logically, more likely to be willing to try other mood-altering drugs than are people who are not willing to try marijuana or who dislike its effects. In other words, many of the factors associated with a willingness to use marijuana are, presumably, the same as those associated with a willingness to use other illicit drugs. Those factors include physiological reactions to the drug effect, which are consistent with the stepping stone hypothesis, but also psychosocial factors, which are independent of drug-specific effects. There is no evidence that marijuana serves as a stepping stone on the basis of its particular physiological effect. One might argue that marijuana is generally used before other illicit mood-altering drugs, in part, because its effects are milder; in that case, marijuana is a stepping stone only in the same sense as taking a small dose of a particular drug and then increasing that dose over time is a stepping stone to increased drug use.

Whereas the stepping stone hypothesis presumes a predominantly physiological component of drug progression, the gateway theory is a social theory. The latter does not suggest that the pharmacological qualities of marijuana make it a risk factor for progression to other drug use. Instead, the legal status of marijuana makes it a gateway drug.

Important Risk Factors

Psychiatric disorders are associated with substance dependence and are probably risk factors for progression in drug use. For example, the troubled adolescents studied by T.J. Crowley and co-workers were dependent on an average of 3.2 substances, and this suggests that their conduct disorders were associated with increased risk of progressing from one drug to another. Abuse of a single substance is probably also a risk factor for later multiple drug use. For example, in a longitudinal study that examined drug use and dependence, about 26% of problem drinkers reported that they first used marijuana after the onset of alcohol-related problems. The study also found that 11% of marijuana users developed chronic marijuana problems; most also had alcohol problems.

Intensity of drug use is an important risk factor in progression. Daily marijuana users are more likely than their peers to be extensive users of other substances. Of 34- to 35-year-old men who had used marijuana 10–99 times by the age 24–25, 75% never used any other illicit drug; 53% of those who had used it more than 100 times did progress to using other illicit drugs 10 or more times. Comparable proportions for women are 64% and 50%.

> *"Social influences, such as peer pressure and prevalence of use by peers, are highly predictive of initiation into marijuana use."*

The factors that best predict use of illicit drugs other than marijuana are probably the following: age of first alcohol or nicotine use, heavy marijuana use, and psychiatric disorders. However, progression to illicit drug use is not synonymous with heavy or persistent drug use. Indeed, although the age of onset of use of licit drugs (alcohol and nicotine) predicts later illicit drug use, it does *not* appear to predict persistent or heavy use of illicit drugs.

Data on the gateway phenomenon are often overinterpreted. For example, one study reports that "marijuana's role as a gateway drug appears to have increased [A. Golub and B.D. Johnson]." It was a retrospective study based on interviews of drug abusers who reported smoking crack or injecting heroin daily. The data from the study provide no indication of what proportion of marijuana users become serious drug abusers; rather, they indicate that serious drug abusers usually use marijuana before they smoke crack or inject heroin. Only a small percentage of the adult population uses crack or heroin daily; during the five-year period from 1993 to 1997, an average of three people per 1,000 used crack and about two per 1,000 used heroin in the preceding month.

> *"Most drug users do not begin their drug use with marijuana—they begin with alcohol and nicotine."*

The Real Issue of the Gateway Discussion

Many of the data on which the gateway theory is based do not measure dependence; instead, they measure use—even once-only use. Thus, they show only that marijuana users are more likely to use other illicit drugs (even if only once) than are people who never use marijuana, not that they become dependent or even frequent users. The authors of these studies are careful to point out that their data should not be used as evidence of an inexorable *causal* progression; rather, they note that identifying stage-based user groups makes it possible to identify the specific risk factors that predict movement from one stage of drug use to the next—the real issue in the gateway discussion.

In the sense that marijuana use typically precedes rather than follows initiation into the use of other illicit drugs, it is indeed a gateway drug. However, it does not appear to be a gateway drug to the extent that it is the *cause* or even that it is the most significant predictor of serious drug abuse; that is, care must be taken not to attribute cause to association. The most consistent predictors of serious drug use appear to be the intensity of marijuana use and co-occurring psychiatric disorders or a family history of psychopathology (including alcoholism).

The Media May Encourage Drug Abuse

by Barry R. McCaffrey

About the author: *Barry R. McCaffrey is the former director of the Office of National Drug Control Policy.*

What we see and hear in the entertainment media influences our beliefs about the world around us. Today's adolescents are deeply immersed in popular culture as it is conveyed through various forms of media. On average, American children are exposed to at least eight hours of media per day including television, radio, movies, recorded music, comics, and video games. The ubiquitous presence of the media in our lives is underscored by the following statistics:

- Ninety-eight percent of American households have a television set. Among households with children, nearly 87 percent have two or more television sets, and 66 percent of American children have a television set in their bedrooms.
- Children spend about 28 hours per week watching television. Over the course of a year, this is twice as much time as they spend in school.
- Sixty-three percent of kids aged 9–17 say that seeing the latest movies is important. Sixty-two percent say that they watch a video at least once a week.
- Between the 7th and 12th grades, American teenagers listen to an estimated 10,500 hours of rock music. More than three-quarters of American youth between the ages of 9–14 watch music videos.
- Eighty-nine percent of teenagers use computers several times per week. Seventy-one percent of young people use computers to play computer games, compared to 47 percent who use them for homework, and 31 percent for education. Teens spend an average of two and one-half hours per day on a home computer.

The Portrayal of Drug Use

Unfortunately, popular culture (including media programming and advertising content) too often portrays drug use as common, something to be expected,

Excerpted from Barry R. McCaffrey's testimony before the United States House of Representatives, House Committee on Appropriations, Subcommittee on Treasury, Postal Service, and General Government, October 21, 1999.

or even humorous. For example, by his or her 18th birthday, an average adolescent will have seen 100,000 television commercials for beer, and will have watched 65,000 scenes on television depicting beer drinking. The Office of National Drug Control Policy (ONDCP)–sponsored Mediascope study Substance Use in Popular Movies and Music examined popular movie rentals and songs to determine the frequency and nature of depictions of substance use (illicit drugs, alcohol, tobacco, and over-the-counter and prescription medicines). The Mediascope study found that 98 percent of movies studied depicted substance use. Illicit drugs appeared in 22 percent. About one-quarter (26 percent) of the movies that depicted illicit drugs contained explicit, graphic portrayals of their preparation and/or ingestion. Less than one half (49 percent) of the movies portrayed short-term consequences of substance use, and about 12 percent depicted long-term consequences. All movies in which illegal drugs appeared received restricted ratings (PG-13 or R). However, 45 percent of the movies in which illicit drugs were used did not receive specific remarks identifying drug-related content from the Motion Picture Association of America. The major finding from the study's song analysis is the dramatic difference among music categories, with substance reference being particularly common in rap. Illicit drugs were mentioned in 63 percent of rap songs versus about 10 percent of the lyrics in the other categories. Neither movies nor music provided much information about motives for substance use. . . .

The Undisputed Influence

The undisputed influence of popular culture on attitude formation and the manner in which it depicts illegal drugs and substance abuse are recognized by the communication strategy that is being implemented by designing the National Youth Anti-Drug Media Campaign. Nearly a year of research went into developing this communication strategy. Hundreds of individuals and organizations were consulted, including experts in teen marketing, advertising, and communication; behavior change experts; drug prevention practitioners; and representatives from professional, civic, and community organizations. These findings resulted in a comprehensive communication strategy that uses a variety of media and messages to reach young people, their parents, and other youth-influential adults. . . .

"Unfortunately, popular culture . . . too often portrays drug use as common, something to be expected, or even humorous."

The Media Campaign's Entertainment Initiative [a five-year initiative, passed in 1998, that aims to reduce youth drug use by deglamorizing drugs in the media] has several major components, all of which are guided by a fundamental philosophy: the entertainment community is a crucial player in addressing substance abuse among teens. They are our partners, and we firmly believe they are part of the solution. We do not subscribe to the widely held view that popular culture is inevitably a destructive force in the area of drugs, and you will not hear this campaign attacking the entertainment community. What you will hear instead is a call for dialogue. We offer information, materials, experts, and a commitment to working together over the long haul. We do not proselytize. We realize that you cannot "shoe horn" a drug message in a script where it does not belong. It must appear organically, and the only way that can be done is if the creative community is aware of the issues and facts. We want true partnerships with key creative people and organizations in order to increase support for the Campaign's fundamental strategic messages. Parent denial, risk perception, peer refusal skills and other message strategies are most effectively communicated by creative talent that is aware of and sensitized to the issues.

Examining Media Content

The Media Campaign's entertainment outreach goals follow:

- Encourage accurate depictions of drug use issues—including the consequences of drug abuse in programming popular with teens and parents.
- Incorporate strategic drug prevention messages and themes into popular culture, and dispel myths and misconceptions about drug abuse.
- De-normalize the image of drug use on TV, and in popular music and film.
- Use entertainment media to provide accurate drug information and resources on substance abuse to parents, caregivers, faith community leaders, and policymakers. . . .

Careful examination of media content is a crucial first step in determining what role media may play in promoting substance use and abuse. The Mediascope study "Substance Use in Popular Movies and Music" . . . is an example of the factual way ONDCP is addressing the issue of the entertainment industry's depiction of illegal drugs. The logic for content analysis is explained by the study's researchers: "if it is true that substance use appears frequently and is portrayed positively in movies and music, then it is reasonable to hypothesize that these portrayals may be influencing young people to use alcohol, tobacco and illicit drugs." And, "if movies and music do contribute to the problem, then, logically, they could also help solve the problem by depicting substance use realistically with consequences, or as deviant, unglamorous, and socially unacceptable.". . .

This generation of adolescents is the most marketed-to generation ever. They are savvy and discriminating about any attempt to persuade them, and could tell you from as early as the age of three which fast food chain has which toy offer, which product is "a rip-off," and which advertising claims over-promise. Anti-drug messages need to be embedded in the social context of kids' popular media culture, through mediums such as programming, in order to complement and authenticate formal ad and education messages.

The Media's Role in Encouraging Drug Abuse Is Exaggerated

by Jacob Sullum

About the author: *Jacob Sullum is a senior editor at* Reason *magazine and author of* For Your Own Good: The Anti-Smoking Crusade and the Tyranny of Public Health.

Like you, I've seen innumerable Calvin Klein ads featuring sallow, sullen, scrawny youths. Not once have I had an overwhelming urge to rush out and buy some heroin, and probably neither have you. Yet the death of Davide Sorrenti, a 20-year-old fashion photographer who overdosed on heroin in February 1997, is now being held up as proof that such images have the power to turn people into junkies.

In May 1997, President Clinton accused the fashion industry of "increasing the allure of heroin among young people" and urged it not to "glamorize addiction" to sell clothes. "We now see on college campuses and in neighborhoods heroin becoming increasingly the drug of choice," he said. "And we know that part of this has to do with the images that are finding their way to our young people."

In reality, heroin is not "the drug of choice" by any stretch of the imagination. In the Government's 1995 National Household Survey on Drug Abuse, 0.1 percent of respondents reported that they had used the drug in the previous month. A nationwide study done in 1994 for the Department of Health and Human Services found about the same level of heroin use among 19- to 28-year-olds; marijuana use was 140 times as common, and alcohol was far and away the most popular intoxicant.

And there is no reason to expect that people attracted to the look promoted by Calvin Klein and other advertisers—a cynical, sanitized vision of drug use that pretends to reflect a gritty reality—will also be attracted to heroin, any more than suburban teen-agers who wear baggy pants and backward caps will end up shooting people from moving cars.

Nevertheless, the editors of the cutting-edge fashion magazines that helped popularize the heroin-chic look are professing repentance. "With Davide's death," said Long Nguyen, *Detour*'s style director, "we realized how powerful fashion pictures are."

And how powerful is that? Leaving aside the point that Mr. Sorrenti, as a producer of these images, can hardly be seen as an unknowing victim of their influence, it is important to keep in mind what pictures can and cannot do. Clearly, they can provoke outrage. They can also pique curiosity, create awareness and elicit a range of emotional reactions. But they cannot *make* anyone buy jeans or perfume, let alone take up heroin. Nor can they make kids smoke cigars, despite the claims of critics about the power of photos showing cigar-chomping celebrities. A conscious mind must intervene, deciding how to interpret the message and whether to act on it.

> *"It is important to keep in mind what pictures can and cannot do. . . . They cannot* **make** *anyone buy jeans or perfume, let alone take up heroin."*

Blurring the distinction between persuasion and coercion is often the first step toward censorship. In the 1950's, John Kenneth Galbraith and Vance Packard argued that corporations used advertising to manipulate consumers and create an artificial desire for their products. The Federal court that upheld the 1970 ban on broadcast advertising of cigarettes was clearly influenced by such ideas, citing "the subliminal impact of this pervasive propaganda."

Flight from Responsibility

We see the same line of thinking today. In calling for restrictions on Web sites promoting alcohol and tobacco, the Center for Media Education, a research group in Washington, warns that "interactivity has a hypnotic and addictive quality that some analysts believe could be stronger than television."

The aim of such arguments is to portray people not as independent moral agents but as mindless automatons. It's a view of human nature that encourages the flight from responsibility to victimhood that we see all around us: the smoker who blames a cigarette maker for his lung cancer, the heavy drinker who blames the liquor company for her baby's birth defects, the mass murderer who blames dirty magazines for inspiring his crimes.

So far no one has called for a ban on glassy-eyed waifs, and the critics of heroin chic have every right to decry the message they believe it sends. But they should be careful not to send a dangerous message themselves: that the dictates of fashion overwhelm our ability to choose.

Chapter 2

Is Drug Abuse a Growing Problem?

Chapter Preface

In the United States, the spreading use of "club drugs" among youths is a growing concern. The term "club drugs" refers to illicit substances frequently found at nightclubs and all-night dance parties known as "raves." Among the most controversial and popular of these drugs is MDMA (methylenedioxymethamphetamine), or "ecstasy," a mildly hallucinogenic stimulant. The drug is prized for the euphoric rush experienced by its users.

Numerous drug abuse experts urgently advise against using ecstasy. Alan I. Leshner, director of the National Institute of Drug Abuse, warns, "Chronic abuse of MDMA appears to produce long-term damage to serotonin-containing neurons in the brain. Given the important role that the neurotransmitter serotonin plays . . . it is likely that MDMA use can cause a variety of behavioral and cognitive consequences as well as impairing memory." Other experts claim that some long-term risks of taking ecstasy have yet to be discovered. For example, one preliminary study suggests that ecstasy abuse can be linked to Parkinson's disease.

However, some contend that the recent studies conducted on ecstasy are inconclusive. Michael Klam, a former ecstasy user, asserts that "no serious science has been done on the kind of periodic dosages of ecstasy I took, a little more than once a month. (In one study, researchers gave monkeys and rats, over four days, an amount of ecstasy equivalent to what I ate in six months.)" Others claim that the deaths and emergencies connected to ecstasy have been hyped by the media, making the drug appear more dangerous than it really is. The Drug Abuse Warning Network reports that in 1998, forty-five hundred drug-related deaths involved cocaine, while deaths associated with ecstasy and other club drugs totaled fifteen.

In the following chapter, the authors offer differing views on trends in the abuse of ecstasy and other drugs in the United States.

Adolescents and Illicit Drug Use

by Ann B. Bruner and Marc Fishman

About the authors: *Ann B. Bruner teaches at the Department of Pediatrics at the Johns Hopkins University School of Medicine, where Marc Fishman teaches at the Department of Psychiatry and Behavioral Sciences.*

Plano, a small Texas community (population, 180,000; median family income, $54,000) just north of Dallas, has been shocked by the deaths of more than 12 adolescents from heroin overdoses during 1997–1998. In Fairfax County, Virginia (population, 900,000; median household income, $70,000), drug-related arrests of adolescents have increased more than 10-fold in 10 years. Across the country parents wonder, "How could it happen to *our* children?" Lifetime prevalence rates of adolescent drug use have been rising since 1992 (Figure 1), and the percentage of teens saying they would never try illegal drugs is decreasing: 86% in 1995, 51% in 1996, and 46% in 1997.

Adolescent substance abuse is an overwhelming public health problem in the United States. In 1997, the lifetime prevalence of any illicit drug use by 12th graders was 54.3%, and approximately one fourth of 10th and 12th graders reported using an illicit substance in the past month. About 76% of high school students and 46% of middle school students say that drugs are kept, used, or sold on school grounds. With 56% of 12- to 17-year-olds reporting that they know a friend or classmate who uses cocaine, heroin, or LSD, it is not surprising that 85% of adolescents cite drugs as the most important problem they face.

Drug use, especially in early adolescence, interferes with normal cognitive, emotional, and social development and is closely linked with both psychiatric disorders and delinquency. Drug use in adolescence has been associated with many other risk-taking behaviors (sexual activity, truancy, violence, or weapon carrying) entailing significant morbidity and mortality (sexually transmitted diseases and human immunodeficiency virus [HIV] infection; pregnancy;

school failure, dropout, or both; injury; suicide and homicide; and motor vehicle crashes). Finally, drug use in adolescence is one of the strongest predictors of lifetime development of drug dependence.

Selected Trends

Tobacco, alcohol, and marijuana are still the most widely abused substances by children and adolescents. Among illicit substances, marijuana has shown an alarming increase in use, especially by younger adolescents. In 1997, 17.7% of 8th graders had used marijuana in the past year, almost 3 times the 1991 rate. The percentage of high school seniors who reported marijuana use in the past month continues to climb, from 13.8% in 1991 to 19.0% in 1994 to 23.7% in 1997. Although marijuana is certainly less toxic than many other drugs, the popular notion that it is harmless is false. Along with its other negative effects, marijuana has a direct effect on short-term memory and other cognitive functions. However, only 58.1% of 12th graders believe that smoking marijuana regularly is harmful, a notable decrease from 1991 (78.6%).

There has also been a dramatic increase in the use of the so-called harder drugs, like heroin, amphetamines, and LSD. Preliminary results from the 1996 National Household Survey on Drug Abuse indicate that the United States is experiencing a heroin epidemic. The estimated number of current heroin users has jumped from 68,000 in 1993 to 216,000 in 1996, and many of these new heroin users are adolescents and young adults. Overall, adolescent use of heroin has nearly doubled since 1991, and 20% of 8th graders report that heroin is readily available to them. The increase in heroin use among adolescents has been associated predominantly with nasal use (snorting or sniffing) rather than use by injection. Global market forces have brought an increasingly higher purity of heroin to the streets, along with greater supplies and cheaper prices ($10 a dose). Heroin purity of less than 5% was the rule 25 years ago, but now purity of 80% to 90% is available. Therefore, nasal administration is effective and efficient, and needles are not necessary. Factors associated with injection drug use that might have kept adolescents away from heroin (needle phobia, social stigma, fear of infection with HIV and/or hepatitis) are not barriers to nasal heroin use. In addition, adolescents may be initially more likely to use nasal heroin because they mistakenly believe that it is safer and less addictive. However, heroin dependence can readily occur with only nasal use. Like nasal cocaine in the 1970s, nasal heroin has become trendy and glamorous. Images of actors, pop stars, and models who use heroin send potent messages ("heroin chic") to adolescents. Both first-time and experienced nasal users risk overdose and death because of the high but variable purity of today's

"Among illicit substances, marijuana has shown an alarming increase in use, especially by younger adolescents."

heroin. Overdose may even be the first clinical presentation of a drug problem in a heroin-using adolescent.

Increasingly Popular Drugs

Methamphetamine (called crystal meth, ice, or crank) is becoming increasingly popular, particularly in the southwest. In 1997, 4.4% of 12th graders had tried this stimulant at least once. At $10 to $30 a dose, methamphetamine is a popular choice for all-night parties ("raves"). Although many people think that LSD, like heroin, is an old-fashioned drug, annual rates of adolescent LSD use are at their highest in 20 years. In 1997, 4.7% of 8th graders and 13.6% of high school seniors had used LSD at least once.

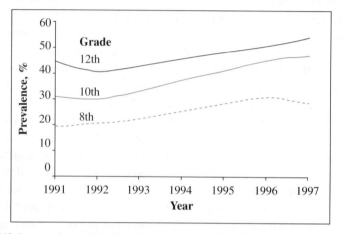

Figure 1. Lifetime prevalence of any illicit drug use, by grade, from Monitoring the Future Study data.

Finally, inhalants (volatile hydrocarbons like toluene, gasoline, solvents, glue, spray paint) remain popular with adolescents. Because of the easy availability of inhalants, inhalant use is most prevalent among younger teens with 5.6% of 8th graders reporting use in the past month; 11.8% use in the past year; and 21.0% lifetime use in 1997. Inhalants can cause seizures, hypoxemia, and fatal arrhythmias in first-time or experienced users. . . .

The Critical Question

What level of drug use by an adolescent constitutes a problem? Experimentation and risk taking are normal aspects of adolescent development, but the idea that experimentation with drugs may be normative is quite problematic. The critical question is whether and to what extent an adolescent's use of substances has caused impairment. [The American Medical Association's 1994] Guidelines for Adolescent Preventive Services (GAPS) recommends that adolescents be asked annually about their drug use. The health care practitioner can then interpret this information in the context of the adolescent's other risk behaviors and overall health.

Home drug test kits ($35 to $60 per kit) have recently become available at grocery stores and pharmacies. A hair or urine specimen can be collected (openly or surreptitiously) and tested for certain drugs of abuse. Advocates for home testing argue that the kits enable families to take control and monitor whether their children are using drugs. Although parents do need to know whether their adolescent is using drugs, drug testing is a clinical procedure that needs to be interpreted in the context of the adolescent's history and examination. The unspoken assumption is that home drug-testing kits adequately test for a drug problem, when in fact a positive test result only represents a snapshot of the recent use of some drugs. Conversely, a negative test result does not imply the absence of drug use or of a drug problem and could give parents a false sense of security. GAPS does not recommend routine urine drug testing. Drug testing is never a substitute for parental monitoring of adolescents, family discussions about drugs, open communication within families, or professional assessment and intervention.

> *"Annual rates of adolescent LSD use are at their highest in 20 years."*

Treatment

Once a drug use problem is identified, treatment resources for adolescents are alarmingly scarce. Substance abuse treatment of adolescents requires a broadened scope of services, including family interventions, mental health care, remedial education, vocational habilitation, and community outreach. The indigent continue to be an underserved population, despite the epidemic of drug use and social devastation in impoverished urban neighborhoods. Furthermore, as managed care spreads into the public sector, there is great concern about its possible detrimental impact on the availability and quality of treatment programs. Even when the considerable barriers to treatment are surmounted, the standards guiding diagnosis and treatment decisions specifically related to adolescents are relatively primitive and often lack empirical verification. However, although there is not enough rigorous adolescent addictions outcomes research, data indicate that treatment is effective. Abstinence or reduction in drug use is sustained in a substantial proportion of adolescents following treatment. Furthermore, posttreatment decreases in amounts and types of drugs used are associated with marked improvements in psychosocial function. Further research is needed to differentiate various treatment models and to test hypotheses concerning which treatments are best suited for which patients.

A Serious and Growing Problem

Adolescent substance abuse is a serious and growing problem in the United States. A greater variety of drugs are available and are less expensive and more dangerous than ever before. Adolescents need effective drug use prevention programs, effective and accessible drug treatment, and enforceable drug interdiction policies linked to mandated treatment. Support for substance abuse education, prevention, and treatment must come from all sides: from families, schools, neighborhood and community groups, policymakers, and health care professionals. Treatment resources for adolescent drug abusers need to be increased, and treatment programs should offer a multifaceted approach that involves a broad coalition of community resources, including juvenile justice and social service agencies, schools, mental health professionals, and primary care clinicians. Our responsibility as health care professionals is to provide vigorous advocacy for our patients by insisting on a greater commitment of resources to drug use prevention and treatment. We must use our expertise to inform the public debate, emphasizing science and data. Finally, we need to expand the scope of research both to improve the effectiveness of treatment in the future and to provide convincing evidence to policymakers that our adolescents desperately need substance abuse treatment now.

Club Drugs Are Harming More Youths

by the Texas Commission on Alcohol and Drug Abuse

About the author: *The Texas Commission on Alcohol and Drug Abuse (TCADA) is a government agency based in Austin, Texas, which provides and funds drug abuse education, prevention, and treatment services.*

Although tobacco and alcohol are the most common substances found on the club scene, other substances such as Ecstasy, Herbal Ecstasy, Rohypnol, GHB, Ketamine, and LSD have gained popularity with young people in recent years. Typically, nightclubs, bars, parties, and raves attract teenagers, college students, and young adults who may risk their health in the interest of a good time. Raves are a form of dance and recreation that is held in a clandestine location with fast-paced high-volume music, a variety of high-tech entertainment, and, often, the use of drugs.

These club drugs are attractive to youth for their cheap, intoxicating highs, which they mistakenly believe are safe. Unfortunately, most partygoers do not realize the dangers of using club drugs. Combinations of any of these drugs with alcohol can lead to unexpected adverse reactions and death.

Ecstasy

Ecstasy or MDMA (methylenedioxymethamphetamine) is a stimulant that combines the properties of methamphetamine or "speed" with mind-altering or hallucinogenic properties. Considered the most commonly used designer drug, Ecstasy is a close derivative of methamphetamine and can be described as a hallucinogenic stimulant. Designer drugs are illicit variations of other drugs. Because of many different recipes used to manufacture Ecstasy, deaths have been caused by some other substances inadvertently created during production, such as PMA (paramethamphetamine). Ecstasy is illegal, and is classified as a Schedule 1 Controlled Substance.

Known on the street as Adam, XTC, Clarity, Essence, Stacy, Lover's Speed,

Excerpted from "Club Drugs: Just the Facts," by the Texas Commission on Alcohol and Drug Abuse, www.tcada.state.tx.us.research, 1997. Reprinted with permission.

Eve, etc., Ecstasy is most often found in tablet, capsule, or powder form and is usually consumed orally, although it can also be injected. Ecstasy is sometimes packaged in capsules or generic tablets to imitate prescription drugs with the average dose costing anywhere from $7 to $30 per pill. Ecstasy can be combined with methadone, LSD, opiates such as heroin or Fentanyl, or strong anesthetics such as Ketamine.

An Ecstasy high can last from six to 24 hours, with the average "trip" lasting only about three to four hours. At moderate doses, Ecstasy is reported to cause euphoria, feelings of well-being, enhanced mental or emotional clarity, anxiety, or paranoia. Heavier doses can cause hallucinations, sensations of lightness and floating, depression, paranoid thinking, and violent, irrational behavior.

Physical reactions can include the following symptoms: loss of appetite, nausea, vomiting, blurred vision, increased heart rate and blood pressure, muscle tension, faintness, chills, sweating, tremors, reduced appetite, insomnia, convulsions, and a loss of control over voluntary body movements. Some reactions have been reported to persist from one to 14 days after taking Ecstasy. Individuals who are pregnant, have a heart condition, are epileptic, or have high blood pressure are at high risk of adverse reactions. In addition, users are at particular risk of heat exhaustion and dehydration with physical exertion, particularly when Ecstasy is taken in a dance-party setting. Deaths have occurred because users don't drink enough water and become overheated.

> *"Ecstasy, Herbal Ecstasy, Rohypnol, GHB, Ketamine, and LSD have gained popularity with young people in recent years."*

Is Herbal Ecstasy a safe, natural alternative? No. Although not currently classified as a controlled substance, Herbal Ecstasy is a drug composed of ephedrine (ma huang) or pseudoephedrine and caffeine (kola nut), stimulants that closely simulate the effects of Ecstasy. Sold in tablet form, Herbal Ecstasy is known as Cloud 9, Herbal Bliss, Ritual Spirit, Herbal X, GWM, Rave Energy, Ultimate Xphoria, and X. There is no quality control over the manufacture of these products, and problems arise because the amounts of ephedrine and caffeine in the pills vary widely. Over 800 reports of adverse reactions such as high blood pressure, seizures, heart attacks, strokes, and death have been reported to federal authorities. Because of these reactions, the Food and Drug Administration (FDA) is considering placing restrictions on the drug.

Rohypnol

Rohypnol (flunitrazepam) is a strong sedative which is manufactured and distributed by Hoffman-La Roche. A member of the benzodiazepine family which includes drugs such as Librium, Xanax, and Valium, Rohypnol is about ten times the strength of Valium. Typically, Rohypnol is smuggled into Texas from the Mexican pharmacias; supplies in Florida come from Latin America. Street prices in Texas range from $1 to $5 per pill. Slang terms for Rohypnol include Roach, Roche (ro-shay), Roofies, Run-Trip-and-Fall, R-2, Mexican Valium, Ropynol, Rib, and Rope. In Texas, to be under the influence of Rohypnol is "to get roached."

Rohypnol is manufactured as small, white tablets with "Roche" inscribed on one side with an encircled "1" or "2" indicating a 1 mg or 2 mg dose. These tablet markings are commonly found on other Roche pharmaceuti-

> *"Club drugs are attractive to youth[s] for their cheap, intoxicating highs, which they mistakenly believe are safe."*

cals, and a pattern of abusing any drug made by Roche (Valium, Klonopin/ Clonopin, Rivotril) has also developed. Rohypnol is usually taken orally, although there are reports that it has been ground up and snorted. Rohypnol is illegal in the United States, and it can draw significant penalties for the possession and sale of the drug.

After taking Rohypnol, the user may feel intoxicated, then sleepy—a feeling that may last up to eight hours. Users under the influence may exhibit slurred speech, impaired judgment, and difficulty walking. Rohypnol can cause deep sedation, respiratory distress, blackouts that can last up to 24 hours, and amnesia where users forget events experienced while under the influence. In some cases, the drug has paradoxical effects and causes users to become aggressive. The potential for overdose or death can occur, especially when mixed with other drugs like alcohol.

GHB

GHB (gamma-hydroxybutyrate) was once sold in health food stores as a performance enhancing additive to body builder formulas. Although rumored that GHB stimulates muscle growth, this claim has never been proven. GHB is a central nervous system depressant that is abused for its intoxicating effects. In 1990, the FDA banned the use of GHB except under the supervision of a physician because of many reports of severe, uncontrollable side effects. Slang terms for GHB include Grievous Bodily Harm, Easy Lay, Gook, Gamma 10, Liquid X, Liquid E, Liquid G, Georgia Home Boy, Soap, Scoop, Salty Water, Somatomax, G-riffick, Cherry Meth, Fantasy, Organic Quaalude, Nature's Quaalude, and Zonked.

GHB is consumed orally in capsule form or as a grainy, white to sandy-colored powder. Powdered GHB is often dissolved in liquids like water or alcoholic beverages and then consumed. However, it is most frequently sold as a slightly salty, clear liquid in small bottles where users pay by the capful or by the teaspoon. Most GHB is created in clandestine laboratories where purity and quality cannot be guaranteed. Often substituted for Ecstasy, another club drug, a capful may cost the user $3 to $5 per dose. GHB is also used as a sedative to come down off stimulants like ephedrine, Ecstasy, speed, or cocaine.

GHB produces intoxication followed by deep sedation. Once ingested, the drug will begin to take effect in 15 minutes to an hour, lasting one to three hours. GHB can cause nausea, vomiting, delusions, depression, vertigo, visual disturbances, seizures, respiratory distress, loss of consciousness, amnesia, and coma. When combined with alcohol and other drugs, the potential for deadly overdoses escalates rapidly. Numerous overdoses in Texas and nationwide have required emergency room treatment and mechanical assistance to breathe.

Ketamine

Ketamine (ketamine hydrochloride) is primarily used in veterinary medicine, and its use as a surgical anesthetic in humans is limited. Most supplies found on the street are diverted from legitimate sources. On the club scene, Ketamine can be found in liquid form or as a white powder that is snorted or smoked with marijuana or tobacco products. A combination of Ketamine and cocaine is called "CK." Other slang terms are Special K, Vitamin K, New Ecstasy, Psychedelic Heroin, Ketalar, Ketaject, and Super-K.

Users experience profound hallucinations and visual distortions similar to the effects of PCP. They call these effects "K-Land." A larger dose can produce a more frightening experience called a "K-hole" or an "out-of-body, near-death experience." They may also experience a loss of senses, sense of time, and identity which can last anywhere from 30 minutes to two hours. Ketamine can cause delirium, amnesia, impaired motor function, high blood pressure, depression, recurrent flashbacks, and potentially fatal respiratory problems.

LSD

LSD (lysergic acid diethylamid) is a potent hallucinogen derived from lysergic acid. Lysergic acid can be found on ergot, a fungus that grows on rye and other grains. Commonly referred to as "acid" on the club scene, a "hit" or dose can be found as tablets, capsules, liquid form, thin squares of gelatin, or absorbed on colorful paper to be licked. Although colorless and odorless, LSD has a slight bitter taste. "Blotter acid," which is absorbent paper soaked in LSD and sold as squares, can be obtained for $4 to $5 for a "high" or "trip" that lasts three to 12 hours. Other slang terms for LSD include Microdot, White Lightning, Blue Heaven, Windowpane, and Sugar Cubes. LSD is a Schedule 1 Controlled Substance with severe penalties for possession and use.

> *"Because of many different recipes to manufacture Ecstasy, deaths have been caused by some other substances inadvertently created during production."*

The effects of LSD are wildly unpredictable depending on a variety of factors. The user will begin to feel the effects within 30 to 90 minutes of ingestion and the "high" may last up to 12 hours. Users under the influence will have dilated pupils, increased body temperature, increased heart and blood pressure rates, loss of appetite, sleeplessness, dry mouth, tremors, and increased perspiration. A "bad trip" could include terrifying thoughts and feelings, fear of losing control, fear of insanity and death, and flashbacks after the fact. Moreover, LSD may reveal long-lasting psychological problems, including schizophrenia and severe depression. Chronic users can develop a tolerance to LSD, meaning they must take more of the drug to feel the same effects.

Unaware of the Dangers

Many young people are introduced to club drugs on the nightclub or rave scene by their peers. People often try drugs like Ecstasy, Herbal Ecstasy, Rohypnol, GHB, Ketamine, and LSD because their friends are using them, and they think that drugs are safe to use.

One major concern about these club drugs is their widespread use among high school youths, college students, and young adults who frequent nightclubs and all-night rave parties. Lured by the availability and intoxicating effects of these drugs, many youths are unaware of the dangers. Rohypnol and GHB, in particular, can cause blackouts and amnesia which place individuals under the influence at risk of sexual assault or other criminal acts. In addition, when young people start using drugs regularly, they often lose interest in school work, which affects academic success as well. Chronic drug use can place students and young adults at risk of dropping out of school or college, loss of employment, and possible encounters with law enforcement.

Heroin Use Has Increased

by Evelyn Nieves

About the author: *Evelyn Nieves is a reporter for the* New York Times.

On January 8, 2001, at 5 A.M. in San Francisco's seedy Tenderloin area, the drug addicts are just about the only ones out.

A young woman with matted blond hair stumbles down the street with her eyes closed; a man in a red spandex dress and silver pumps nods out against the door of a single-room-occupancy hotel; small clusters of hollow-eyed men and women hover on corners. It is no wonder the police call this strip of the Tenderloin the heroin corridor. Everyone on the street looks either high or hung over.

Later in the day, Matt Dodman, a blond, angelic-looking 26-year-old, is sitting in a cafe in another, hipper neighborhood, the Mission. A heroin user for three years, he avoids the Tenderloin drug scene. "I'm not part of a hard-core drug clique," he said, taking a sip of mineral water. But down the block, a dozen of his friends and acquaintances—all heroin addicts in their teens and 20's, and all disheveled and homeless, as he is—sit on the sidewalk outside a community center and wait to be tested for hepatitis C. More than half will test positive, just as in the larger population of San Francisco heroin users who have been taking the drug at least five years.

Yesterday's Drug?

Heroin was supposed to be over, yesterday's drug. But almost 20 years after AIDS made injecting it deadlier than it had ever been, it is as common in some neighborhoods here as Starbucks. A draw for drug experimenters since the heyday of Haight-Ashbury, the city remains a place where "old" heroin addicts—those who have been using the narcotic for 20 or 25 years—feed their habit. But more and more young people as well are using it.

And not just here. Hospitals and treatment centers in other large cities, especially in the West, are seeing record numbers of heroin cases. Chicago officials attribute a surge in life-threatening cases of asthma to increased use of heroin among the young. And while H.I.V. and AIDS are down among users, needles used to inject heroin are responsible for an increase in hepatitis C, which can cause liver failure. In fact, hepatitis C is growing across the United States and in Vancouver, British Columbia, a major trafficking point for a drug pipeline that extends from Canada to California.

The estimated number of heroin users in the United States has risen to 980,000 from 600,000 at the beginning of the 1990's, while cocaine use has decreased 70 percent, according to the White House Office of National Drug Control Policy. The agency attributes the resurgence in heroin use to new forms of the drug, smokable and snortable alike; to a prevailing myth among the young that heroin is safer when not injected; and to the "heroin chic" look of models in the early 90's.

Washington State, Oregon and California have the highest incidence of heroin abuse in the West. Elsewhere, New York, New Jersey, Michigan, Massachusetts and Delaware also have big problems with it, according to the Substance Abuse and Mental Health Services Administration, an agency of the Department of Health and Human Services. Dr. H. Westley Clark, the agency's director, says its household surveys show that from 1996 to 1998, an estimated 471,000 people used heroin for the first time, with a quarter of the new users under 18 and 47 percent age 18 to 25.

Big Increase

Heroin is not only cheaper than it once was, "it's cleaner, purer," said Joseph A. Califano Jr., who was secretary of health, education and welfare in the Carter administration and now directs the Center for Addiction and Substance Abuse at Columbia University. "And too many young people think they can snort it and they won't get hooked." Eventually, Mr. Califano added, they do get hooked, and turn to needles to achieve a more potent high.

"The next drug czar, in the [George W.] Bush administration, is going to have to deal with heroin in a big way," he said.

Public health experts see the big increase in heroin use as further evidence that the nation's 20-year-old

> *"Heroin was supposed to be over, yesterday's drug."*

war on drugs, with its emphasis on punishment rather than addict treatment, needs a new approach.

Here in San Francisco, heroin users, like homeless people (many are both), are part of the landscape. The city draws young people with troubled backgrounds from all over the country, even as it tries coping with inveterate users who have lived on the streets for years.

The new people, like Matt Dodman, from Michigan, arrive with no money and no plans. Often they end up in loose-knit communities of homeless drug users, scorned by the rest of the city and consumed with a need to get their fixes. People cross the street to avoid them. "They look at us like dogs," Mr. Dodman said.

To support his habit, which costs him $20 to $30 a day, Mr. Dodman steals. Or he "boosts"—steals an item from a store, then returns it for cash. He has panhandled, but says he does not "have the patience for it."

Dr. David E. Smith, founder and president of the Haight-Ashbury Free Clinics, drug treatment centers here, has described the city's young addict population as people looking for "geographical cheer"—hope that life is

> *"The estimated number of heroin users in the United States has risen to 980,000 from 600,000 at the beginning of the 1990's."*

going to be better in San Francisco than it was in Des Moines or wherever. Instead, they become alienated. The same is true of neighborhoods that attract young transients in Seattle and Portland. Officials in both cities consider heroin use at epidemic levels. In 1999, Portland had the nation's highest rate of death from heroin overdose.

"You look back into the early 90's, and the heroin deaths are one to two dozen per year, and then in 1999 it was 111," said Gary Oxman, director of the Multnomah County Health Department in Portland. The department expects the final number for 2000 to drop to the low to middle 70's, he said, in part because of aggressive education programs.

Stepping Up Efforts

San Francisco has stepped up efforts in recent years to divert drug users to treatment. Such programs are making the city a model for California now that a statewide voter initiative, to take effect on July 1, 2000, makes first-time drug offenders eligible for treatment rather than jail. But more people keep coming to San Francisco than the city can help.

Matt Dodman was one of several addicts, young and old alike, who said in interviews on the streets that they could not find a program that would accept them. Another was R.J., who said he had been using heroin for 40 of his 49 years and could not find a space in the city's detoxification centers.

R.J., who would identify himself only by his initials, saying he wanted to spare his four children, is a walking sign of what heroin can cost. He has overdosed five times. He has been stabbed and raped while selling himself to support his habit. He has done time behind bars, almost nine years in all. And his inner forearms have so many needle tracks that they look striped.

By selling his body, R.J. earns enough money to pay for his heroin, if nothing else. "When I see young people, I tell them, 'Don't end up like me,'" he said. "I tell them, 'Look at me.'"

Gloria Clay, like R.J. a Tenderloin regular, is a little luckier. At 35, she is in a detoxification program and says she is on her way to kicking a heroin habit she picked up in 1999, after being addicted to crack.

Her scars keep her motivated. While on drugs, she was kicked by her drug-addicted boyfriend, a beating that cost her an eye and permanently damaged her spine.

The Long-Term Effects

Although infected sores in heroin addicts are the leading cause of admissions at San Francisco General Hospital, and while San Francisco consistently ranks among the worst metropolitan areas for emergency-room visits related to heroin, health officials here are more worried about the drug's long-term effects.

Experts compare heroin users to smokers, in that risk accumulates over time. Many people infected with the hepatitis C virus, for example, do not exhibit symptoms for many years, said Dr. Andrew Moss, professor in residence of epidemiology and biostatistics at the University of California at San Francisco. But, Dr. Moss said, a segment of those afflicted will develop liver disease, cancer or cirrhosis, and hepatitis C is very infectious.

In San Francisco, where young users as well as old overdose routinely, the young are very difficult to reach, because their problems transcend drug use, Dr. Moss said. "They're America's damaged children," he said.

Matt Dodman is not worried. He is sure he will not overdose, and certain he will remain free of disease. Why? "Because," he said, "I know so."

Hallucinogens Are Harmful

by Kathiann M. Kowalski

About the author: *Kathiann M. Kowalski is a writer of children's books and the author of* Teens Rights: At Home, at School, Online.

Drugs that play havoc with your brain can totally mess up your life.

"You've got to help me," Raphael said, grabbing the emergency room doctor's arm. "The leprechauns are everywhere."

Restraining the terrified teen took five people. The "friend" who'd dropped Raphael off in the hospital parking lot didn't stick around to tell anyone what he'd taken. Meanwhile, the boy's heart raced at more than 160 beats per minute. His skin was flushed and dry. Within minutes, he went into seizures.

Finally a doctor with special toxicology training connected Raphael's rantings about little people to the hallucinogen jimsonweed. With no time to spare, the ER team gave Raphael medicine that saved his life.

Raphael's immediate emergency is over for now, but chances are he may continue to use hallucinogens. For many young people, hallucinogens remain a repeated threat.

Trips: Distorted Reality

Hallucinogens are drugs that cause hallucinations—the perception of something that isn't there. Hallucinogens also cause changes in thought and mood. Oddly, most users are aware that what they sense isn't real, but is drug-induced.

Some hallucinogen experiences, or trips, produce weird illusions. One user claimed he saw hordes of jabbering creatures "juggling incandescent neon microworlds."

Intensified sensations, such as brighter colors or louder sounds, occur in other trips. Still other trips bring a distorted sense of space and time. Users may feel like they're floating outside their bodies.

Another odd effect of hallucinogens is synesthesia. In synesthesia, senses get "cross-wired." Users think they can see sounds or smell colors.

The weirdness can turn into horror. Sara took the hallucinogen ketamine. Afterward, the 16-year-old thought everyone dancing on the floor with her was decapitated. The image was gruesome.

One LSD user saw a giant lizard chewing a woman's neck. The plain carpet beneath his feet seemed to be a blood-soaked sponge. Still other hallucinogen users have reported sensations of being probed by slimy fingers or pulled down by grasping tentacles.

Terror and panic from bad trips breed paranoia—the irrational fear that everyone is after you. One high school sophomore felt so afraid after taking LSD that he ran screaming through fields in rural Michigan. Another LSD user threatened to attack his friend with a knife.

Abuse of hallucinogens surged during the 1960s and 1970s. During the 1980s, hallucinogen use dropped, but then it rose again in the '90s. The 1999 Monitoring the Future Study by researchers at the University of Michigan surveyed teen drug use. It found that about 14 percent of 12th graders had used hallucinogens at some point. The dramatic rise in usage rates—over 46 percent since 1991—raises serious health issues.

Natural and Synthetic Varieties

More than 100 chemicals are known hallucinogens. Some, like the jimsonweed Raphael took, come from plants. Jimsonweed contains the drug atropine. Its name comes from colonial Jamestown, where settlers became very ill after mistakenly eating it in a salad.

Peyote cactus buttons contain the drug mescaline. So-called magic mushrooms contain psilocybin and psilocin. One type of morning glory seed also produces hallucinogens.

Hallucinogens come from animals too. Certain toads secrete bufotenine. Besides distorting reality, the chemical causes high blood pressure, rapid heartbeat, blurred vision, and cramped muscles.

More potent hallucinogens come from laboratories. Using extracts from rye fungus, Swiss chemist Albert Hoffman developed LSD (lysergic acid diethylamide) in 1938. Also called acid, LSD was reported to be used by 13 percent of the 12th graders in the University of Michigan study. Less than 0.001 gram of LSD produces extreme hallucinations. LSD takes effect within 30 minutes. It lasts about 12 hours.

Another chemist, Alexander Shulgin, developed STP, or DOM (2,5-dimethoxy-4-methylamphetamine). The drug is over 50 times more potent than mescaline.

Other synthetic hallucinogens include DMA (dimethyloxyamphetamine), MDA (methylenedioxyamphetamine), and DMT (dimethyltryptamine). DMT's effects peak within minutes and usually wear off within an hour.

"For many young people, hallucinogens remain a repeated threat."

PCP (phencyclidine) is highly unpredictable. Some users feel out of touch with their bodies and surroundings. Others get so revved up they become violent. Because PCP is also an anesthetic, it deadens users' sense of pain. PCP's nicknames include angel dust, rocket fuel, and ozone.

The veterinary anesthetic ketamine is also called Special K, Kit Kat, green, and blind squid. Because it's chemically like PCP, ketamine has similar effects.

Then there are a host of "designer drugs." Some produce distorted sensations and have other effects too. MDMA (methylenedioxymethamphetamine), or Ecstasy, first became popular in the 1980s at all-night parties called raves. Besides producing out-of-body sensations, Ecstasy is a powerful stimulant. Overdoses have killed young people.

Mind-Altering Drugs

How do hallucinogens work? The answers lie inside the brain.

Neurotransmitters are naturally produced chemicals. They carry messages between different nerve cells. Specific parts of nerve cells, called receptors, respond to specific neurotransmitters. To bind at a receptor, a chemical must fit just right—like a tiny jigsaw puzzle.

Serotonin, or 5-HT, is one neurotransmitter. It plays a role in sleep, memory, learning, mood, and behavior. It also affects body temperature, cardiovascular function, hormone secretion, and possibly pain sensation.

> *"The dramatic rise in [hallucinogen] usage rates—over 46 percent since 1991—raises serious health issues."*

Fourteen kinds of receptors respond to serotonin. But LSD and similar hallucinogens (called classical hallucinogens) bind to only one group of these receptors, called 5HT-2 receptors. This selective binding to only some serotonin receptors seems to be what triggers the drugs' hallucinogenic effects.

Mind-altering drugs that aren't classified with LSD affect different receptors. PCP, for example, appears to interfere with receptors for the neurotransmitter glutamate. It may also affect receptor sites for dopamine. Dopamine is linked to feelings of pleasure.

Scientists know that hallucinogens stimulate particular receptors in the brain. Exactly how that produces different types of hallucinations, however, remains largely a mystery. "We don't know exactly what's going on," admits Robert Findling at University Hospitals in Cleveland, Ohio. "We believe that hallucinations are a result of abnormal brain activity. Different parts of the brain become activated when they shouldn't."

No one can predict when a hallucinogen user will have a bad trip. Dosage, the specific drug, and the setting in which it's taken all affect the user's experience. The bottom line, however, is that hallucinogens are unpredictable. That unpredictability makes them dangerous.

There's no effective treatment for a bad trip. Only having the drug wear off will make imagined demons go away. Books and articles recommend trying to calm distressed users in a quiet, uncrowded spot. But friends who are high themselves can't be counted on for help.

Flashbacks are even scarier. A flashback is a relived experience from a halluci-nation. Both frequent users and one-time experimenters can find themselves on another trip when they least expect it, such as while a teen is driving a car or performing gymnastics.

> *"Hallucinogens are unpredictable. That unpredictability makes them dangerous."*

Flashbacks can suddenly bring back feelings of terror and paranoia. One young woman's flashback was so intense that she jumped out the window in a high-rise apartment building. The flashback came six months after her single experience with LSD.

Some hallucinogen users have needed treatment for serious psychological problems, as well as for their drug abuse. In certain instances, hallucinogen abuse seems to "unmask" preexisting psychological problems. Instead of re-solving the underlying problem, however, hallucinogens only complicate things and add the additional problems that come with drug abuse.

Ongoing Risks

Different hallucinogenic drugs affect the brain's receptors in different ways, with varying effects. Users may think they need the drugs to escape the pres-sures of day-to-day living. Or, they may continue taking the drug because their whole group uses hallucinogens. Whatever the reason, continued use means on-going risks from the drugs.

Users also develop a tolerance to hallucinogens over time. In other words, they need more of the drugs to get the same effects. Higher doses greatly in-crease the risks of a bad trip and troubling flashbacks.

Complicating matters even more is the fact that hallucinogen users often abuse other drugs too, especially marijuana. Those other drugs bring along all their own physical and psychological risks, including the danger of addiction.

Hallucinogens don't just mess with the mind. They have physical effects too, such as dilated pupils, warm skin, and excessive sweating.

LSD, Ecstasy, and most other hallucinogens increase heart rate and blood pressure, which can lead to sleeplessness and tremors. Overdoses can result in convulsions, coma, and heart and lung failure.

Users in the throes of a bad trip may hurt themselves. Some commit suicide to escape the trip's terrors. One study from the *Journal of Pediatrics* reported that 20 percent of adolescent hallucinogen users knew someone who'd had a suicide attempt or accident because of the drugs.

Incoherent speech, impaired coordination, and decreased awareness of touch and pain go along with many hallucinogens. Users also experience feelings of detachment and invincibility. After someone spiked her drink with PCP, 22-year-old Naomi wandered across town in icy cold weather without a coat. Cars barely missed hitting Naomi as she wandered. Later, she pondered jumping off a bridge. Naomi recalled feeling certain that nothing bad could happen to her.

Drownings, burns, falls, and motor vehicle crashes bring thousands of hallucinogen users to hospital emergency rooms each year. Sadly, many don't survive their hallucinogen-induced injuries. Violent behavior associated with hallucinogens lands other users in jail.

Specific hallucinogens may have their own toxic effects. Peyote can cause nausea. Mushroom users run the risk that collectors mistakenly picked toxic toadstools instead.

Long-term effects are a separate issue. A 1999 study by researchers at Johns Hopkins University suggests that Ecstasy harms brain cells. The full implications of the findings are not yet known. Of course, pregnant women who use hallucinogens or any other drugs risk harming their unborn children.

Long-term effects aren't limited to specific diseases, however. Paralysis from an accident, a criminal record, and severe psychological problems can ruin a teen's life. "These are bad, dangerous drugs," stresses Dr. Findling. "These can profoundly alter the course of a [teen's] life for the worse."

In Your Right Mind

Advocates of hallucinogen use from the 1960s claimed that the drugs could help harness creativity. Hallucinogens, however, are merely temporary tricks that affect the mind. "You're tricking your mind to see things that aren't there," warns Dr. Findling. "You end up doing things that you're not supposed to."

Indeed, people who hallucinate without taking drugs aren't society's creative geniuses. They're people with serious psychological problems. They don't function normally and need professional help. "You wouldn't want to do that to yourself," says Dr. Findling.

Instead of "dropping out," choose to live your life in the real world. Set realistic goals for yourself, and work toward them. Get involved with friends and family. Do activities that are important to you. Avoid hallucinogens, alcohol, and other drugs too. Then you can stay in touch with all your thoughts and perceptions. There's no better way to stimulate your creative spirit.

Playing with Painkillers

by Claudia Kalb et al.

About the author: *Claudia Kalb is associate editor of* Newsweek, *a weekly American newsmagazine, and reports on health care issues.*

It all started innocently enough. Three years ago, when Michelle Brown got pregnant, her doctor wrote her a prescription for Lortab, a potentially addictive painkiller similar to Vicodin, for relief from migraine headaches. Her migraines eventually got worse; the Lortab made her life bearable. But it had a devastating side effect: "Slowly," says Brown, who is from Sanford, Maine, "I started to get addicted." She became a classic "doctor shopper," hopping from one physician to the next to get multiple prescriptions. She discovered Percocet, and soon she was mixing Lortab with OxyContin, a new, superstrength painkiller she got through a dealer. By early last year, Brown, 25 years old, and the mother of two small children, worked up the nerve to commit fraud. Pretending to be phoning from her doctor's office, she called her local pharmacy, read her physician's identification number off a prescription bottle and won, she says, "my key to the palace."

For millions of Americans, painkillers are a godsend. Cancer patients suffer the agony a little bit more easily. People battling severe arthritis can, for the first time, take walks and play with their grandchildren. Realizing that for years doctors neglected to include pain management in patient care, the medical establishment has, over the past decade, taken a new, more aggressive approach to treating pain. In January a national accrediting board issued new standards requiring doctors in hospitals and other facilities to treat pain as a vital sign, meaning that they must measure it and treat it as they would blood pressure or heart rate. Even Congress has gotten into the act, last fall passing a law declaring the next 10 years the "Decade of Pain Control and Research."

In this environment, pharmaceutical companies are experimenting with new formulations of painkillers, and existing painkillers themselves are more widely distributed than ever before. While the pharmaceutical market doubled to $145 billion between 1996 and 2000, the painkiller market tripled to $1.8 billion over the same period. Yet at the same time, the incidence of reported first-time abuse of painkillers has also surged. Many of these painkillers aren't new, and "there's not necessarily something wrong with" the increase in controlled substances, says Michael Moy in the Drug Enforcement Administration's Office of Diversion Control. "But once you put something into the food chain, someone's going to want to bite."

Although there are no perfect statistics on how many people misuse or abuse prescription drugs, in 1999 an estimated 4 million Americans over the age of 12 used prescription pain relievers, sedatives and stimulants for "nonmedical" reasons in the past month, with almost half saying they'd done so for the first time. According to the DEA, the most-abused prescription drugs include the oxycodone and hydrocodone types of painkillers, which contain potentially addictive opioids (the two drugs differ slightly in chemical structure, but both work similarly on the body). And emergency-room data suggest that certain drugs have seen dramatic spikes in abuse in recent years. ER visits involving hydrocodone medications like Vicodin and Lortab jumped from an estimated 6,100 incidents in 1992 to more than 14,000 in 1999, oxycodone painkillers like Percodan and OxyContin rose from about 3,750 to 6,430 and the anti-anxiety drug Xanax (including generic formulations) increased from 16,500 to more than 20,500. Illegal drugs, abused in much higher numbers, also increased: cocaine from 120,000 to 169,000 and heroin and morphine from 48,000 to 84,400.

Reports of painkiller abuse from Hollywood catch the attention of the public more than any statistic ever will. In the last six months, Melanie Griffith and Matthew Perry each checked into rehab, publicly acknowledging their addiction to prescription painkillers. TV shows fill their scripts with the problem: on "ER," Dr. John Carter gets hooked on painkillers after he's stabbed, and on the new show, "The Job," Denis Leary plays a detective who takes painkillers on a stakeout. Even Homer Simpson battles a compulsion for the drugs in a season-ender where he's catapulted into a surreal celebrity existence. After looking at the data and following the news reports, the National Institute on Drug Abuse (NIDA) will announce next week a major public-health initiative about prescription-drug abuse. "Once you get into millions of people [abusing]," says Dr. Alan Leshner, NIDA's director, "you have a serious public-health issue on your hands."

Addiction to prescription drugs is not a new problem. Remember "Valley of the Dolls"? The uppers, the downers, the sleeping pills? But some of today's drugs are far more

> *"In 1999 an estimated 4 million Americans over the age of 12 used prescription pain relievers . . . for 'nonmedical' reasons in the past month."*

sophisticated than anything Jacqueline Susann could have envisioned. OxyContin, which hit the market in 1996, is by far the most powerful: it's a 12-hour time-release incarnation of the molecular compound oxycodone, the active ingredient in older drugs like Percodan and Percocet. Unlike drugs in the hydrocodone category, OxyContin and several other oxycodones don't contain acetaminophen, which can damage the liver in high doses and limits the extent to which those drugs can be safely used. OxyContin allows patients to swallow fewer pills, and offers pain relief three times longer than earlier versions. But when the drug is crushed and snorted, eliminating its time-release feature, it's a huge narcotic rush to the brain. "You feel vitalized, like you can do whatever you want," says Eric, 38, of Portland, Maine, who has spent as much as $525 a week buying the drug from a street dealer. Abuse of OxyContin has gotten so bad that in some areas users are robbing pharmacies to get the drug—just last month, Hannaford, a major chain in Maine, decided that "for the safety of our associates and customers," it would no longer stock the drug on its shelves.

When it comes to prescription painkillers, there is no typical abuser. Police departments say they've seen every variety, from teenagers to stay-at-home moms to executives who started taking drugs for their tennis elbow. Particularly at risk are chronic substance abusers who may divert to prescription drugs when their preferred poisons, like heroin, run out. In Hollywood clubs, cocaine and ecstasy still dominate, one 30-year-old actor says, but people also share Vicodin, Xanax and Valium, then wash them down with alcohol. Health-care professionals, with easy access to drugs, often succumb. Among arrests in Cincinnati, which carefully tracks prescription-drug abuse, 30 percent of cases involve medical employees.

> *"Addiction to prescription drugs is not a new problem."*

Landon Gibbs, a Virginia state police officer, says his department arrested a doctor last year who would "write a prescription, drive that person to the pharmacy and then split the pills."

Prescription painkillers are appealing in part because users think of them as "safe." They're FDA approved, easy to take on the sly and don't have the same stigma as illegal drugs. Cindy Mogil started taking Valium at 20 to ease the trauma after a car accident, and "liked the feeling of euphoria." As a manager in a health clinic, she had easy access to sample pills, then found her way to Vicodin and Percodan, visiting different doctors to get her supply. "Boy, it's so easy," says Mogil, who lives in suburban Atlanta. "I'd walk in and tell them I had a migraine; that's all I had to say." Her family never questioned the pills: "They think you're taking it for medical reasons." Finally, after two decades of abuse, Mogil collapsed—her face numb, her speech slurred—and checked into rehab. "I was no better than a street addict," she says.

All pain passes through the brain. Pills like Vicodin and OxyContin lock onto a cell receptor called mu, found most prominently in the brain, spinal cord and gut. When the drug connects to the receptors in the spinal cord, pain signals from nerves are blocked; in the brain, the receptors seem to promote an overall sense of well-being; in the gut, they have the unfortunate side effect of constipation. While any patient who takes an opioid painkiller or any other addictive drug over a long period will develop a physical dependence—meaning the body adjusts to the chemicals now swirling about and thinks that's normal—that dependence can be properly managed. When it's time to go off the drug, a good physician will taper the prescription so there's no withdrawal or rebound effect. But a genetic tendency, an underlying mental illness, a

> *"When it comes to prescription painkillers, there is no typical abuser."*

history of substance abuse or a combination of factors may lead a small group of patients to go beyond just physical dependence. They become compulsive about taking the drug, even when it threatens their health or social and professional lives.

Once you're hooked, getting more becomes an obsession. Many abusers, like Michelle Brown, become doctor shoppers. Others buy their fix on the street: one Vicodin goes for about $6, Percocet and Percodan, up to $8, and an 80mg OxyContin for as much as $80. Tales of cunning and desperation abound—the weekend visits to the ER claiming a toothache, the stolen prescription pads. Dr. Sheila Calderon, an internist in Dallas, says a former employee used her name to call in a prescription for Vicodin (she was never charged). Cathy Napier, a former Percodan addict and now head of the chemical-dependency program at Presbyterian Hospital in Dallas, says she knows women who go to real-estate open houses, "then go through the medicine cabinets and steal the Lortab."

So who's to blame for the misuse of these drugs? Many abusers point the finger at doctors, who they say tend to prescribe medications too quickly without warning patients that certain drugs can be highly addictive. But once patients begin deceiving doctors and pharmacists by phoning in fake scripts or seeking prescriptions from multiple doctors, they become the culprits. Seventeen states currently have prescription-monitoring programs, which vary widely—some track drugs like OxyContin (a schedule II drug, deemed "high potential for abuse"), but not Vicodin (schedule III, "some potential"). But many states don't dedicate resources to full-time oversight. Nor does the DEA, which is largely watching out for abuse by health professionals. If abusers are caught, they're charged with fraud—a misdemeanor in some states and a felony in others. Brown says she is "so thankful" for the DEA agent who handled her case after a suspicious pharmacist called the police. "He knew I needed help. He told my family everything. And it just blew open from there." Now, says Brown, she's in treatment, taking methadone to ease her off her addiction and finally "learning how to live a normal life."

With all the focus on abusers, pain specialists worry that legitimate patients will suffer. Too many doctors succumb to "opiophobia," fear of prescribing much-needed medications for appropriate patients who suffer moderate to severe pain, says Dr. Russell Portenoy, chair of pain medicine at New York's Beth

Israel Medical Center. Dr. Kenneth Pollack, a pain specialist in Des Moines, Iowa, says he recently prescribed OxyContin for a woman who had suffered painful nerve tumors in her feet for 11 years and could barely stand up. Last time Pollack saw her, "she was practically in tears," he says. "She said, 'Thank you for giving me my life back.'" Says David E. Joranson, director of the Pain & Policy Studies Group at the University of Wisconsin: "My fear is that some patients and doctors are going to start looking at this stuff like it's nuclear material. There is a real risk of losing recent gains made in pain management."

Pharmaceutical companies acknowledge that misuse is a problem. Pharmacia, which manufactures Xanax, says "all of our peer-group companies realize there is a potential for abuse here." They say they educate as many people as possible about the importance of taking the drug safely under a doctor's care; the drug is also marketed generically by other companies. Abbott Labs, which manufactures Vicodin, offers symposiums for prescribers and pharmacists to teach about abuse potential. And Purdue Pharma, which manufactures OxyContin, has been actively addressing the problem through education sessions and meetings with the DEA and the FDA.

Maryann Timmons, 51, says she needs her medication. After lifelong ear infections and a broken eardrum, Timmons, 51, of Concord Township, Ohio, takes Vicodin to dull the pain. Initially, she says, her doctor didn't want to prescribe the pills; he ultimately did, but told Timmons to use them sparingly because of their addictive potential. "I felt like a criminal," she says. "It shouldn't be a battle to get help with pain relief." Pain relief and criminal activity. The new challenge for doctors and public-health officials is to provide one without advancing the other.

Drug Abuse Among Youths Has Not Increased

by the Civic Research Institute

About the author: *The Civic Research Institute (CRI) is an independent publisher of reference and practice materials for professionals in criminal justice, health, social, and legal services.*

The National Household Survey on Drug Abuse has been conducted annually since 1975 by the Institute for Social Research at the University of Michigan under a grant from the National Institute on Drug Abuse. The 1998 survey was based on a nationally representative sample of 25,500 respondents age 12 and older. . . . The survey covers an extensive range of behaviors, and allows researchers to produce national estimates of current and lifetime substance use among different segments of the population, and to analyze trends over time. The preliminary results from the 1998 National Household Survey on Drug Abuse are reported in the *Summary of Findings from the 1998 National Household Survey on Drug Abuse (Summary of Findings Report)*.

The sample population for the National Household Survey on Drug Abuse does not include the homeless or those who are institutionalized (e.g., in correctional institutions or residential drug treatment facilities), and drug use rates tend to be high among these missed populations. Among the survey respondents, some degree of underreporting is assumed. The use rates yielded from the survey, especially for drugs such as heroin and cocaine, must be considered underestimates of the actual rates for the entire population.

Downturn in Youth Drug Use Seen

According to the *Summary of Findings Report*, the total estimated number of current illicit drug users in the U.S. did not change from 1997 to 1998. There was a significant decrease, however, in the number of drug users among the 12 to 17 age group: 9.9% of youths in this age group reported drug use in 1998, compared to 11.4% in 1997. This represents the first statistically significant downturn in youth drug use as recorded by the survey since 1992, when only 5.3% of the youth surveyed reported past month use of any illicit drug. One note about statistical significance: The 1998 survey included 6,778 respondents in the age 12 to 17 group. With large samples, relatively small changes in drug use rates from one year to another may be statistically significant. Therefore, while a 1.5% decrease in the percentage of teenagers using illicit drugs may appear trivial, this decrease amounts to hundreds of thousands *fewer* teens using drugs in 1998 compared to 1997. The 1998 survey results are important because even small significant decreases may be reliable indicators of a downturn in drug use. (In the remainder of this article, all percentages from the survey are rounded to whole numbers.)

According to the *Summary of Findings Report*, the 1998 data "show that overall drug use remained level, and the rate of drug use among youths fluctuated and may have also leveled or possibly started to decrease after a period of increase from 1992 to 1995." The recent National Household Survey results are also consistent with the results of other national surveys which show a leveling off of drug use among youths.

Use of Drugs Other than Marijuana Is Rare

Among the entire survey population, 6% were current (past month) illicit drug users, the same percentage reported since 1992. Regular illicit drug use in 1998 was essentially unchanged from the 1997 survey figures among the 18 to 25 age group (16% reported use in 1998), the 26 to 34 age group (7% reported use in 1998), and the over 35 group (3% reported use in 1998).

Among the entire population, 5% reported regular use of marijuana. Less than 3% of the population reported past month use of any illicit drug other than marijuana. Marijuana is the most commonly used illicit substance, and is used by 81% of all current drug users. About 40% of current drug users were users of an illicit drug other than marijuana. While an estimated 13.6 million Americans were current users of illicit drugs in 1998, only 1.8 million (2% of the population) reported regular use of cocaine. This percentage has remained relatively stable since 1992. In 1998, less than 1% of the survey population reported regular use of crack, heroin, LSD, or inhalants. Among youths age 12 to 17, regular use of cocaine, inhalants, hallucinogens, and heroin by juveniles was very low (1% to 2%) and essentially unchanged from the 1997 survey figures (exception: inhalant use fell from 2% to 1%).

"9.9% of youths [age 12 to 17 years] . . . reported drug use in 1998, compared to 11.4% in 1997."

For the population as a whole, regular illicit drug use in 1998 was higher among blacks (8%) than among whites (6%) and Hispanics (6%), and higher among men (8%) than among women (5%). . . .

Among youths age 12 to 17, rates of past month use of any illicit drug did not vary by race or gender, although regular alcohol use was higher among white youths (21%), than among hispanics (19%), or blacks (13%). Drug use was higher in rural areas than in non-rural areas. Among youths age 12 to 17, for example, 11% of rural youth and 8% of non-rural youth reported past month drug use in 1998.

Drug Use Correlates with Education and Employment

Among those in the 26 to 34 age group, regular illicit drug use is highest among those who have not completed high school (10%) and lowest among college graduates (5%). Among respondents age 18 and older, drug use was much lower for individuals who were employed full-time (6%) than among the unemployed (18%); however, most adult drug users (73%) were employed. In contrast to the patterns for drug use, regular use of alcohol is highest among college graduates (66%) and lowest among those who did not complete high school (40%). Past month binge and heavy drinking was less prevalent among college graduates.

Drugs Easy for Youths to Obtain

Over half of the 1998 survey respondents age 12 to 17 said that marijuana was easy to obtain, 30% said it was easy to obtain cocaine, and 21% said it was easy to obtain heroin. These percentages were even higher for the population at large (age 12 and over). Fourteen percent of youths age 12 to 17 said they had been approached by someone selling drugs in the past month. The percentage of youths who believe that regular use of cigarettes, alcohol, or drugs involves "great risk" remained unchanged in 1998.

There Is No Adolescent Heroin Crisis

by Mike Males

About the author: *Mike Males is a freelance writer and author of* The Scapegoat Generation: America's War on Adolescents *and* Framing Youth: Ten Myths About the Next Generation.

1970: "Kids and Heroin: The Adolescent Epidemic," trumpeted *Time* (3/16/70). "A terrifying wave of heroin use among youth . . . has caught up teenagers and even pre-adolescent children from city ghettos to fashionable suburbs." Quoting unnamed "experts," *Time* predicted the number of teenage heroin addicts in New York "may mushroom fantastically to 100,000 this summer. . . . Disaster looms large."

Although exaggerated, 1970s fears had some foundation. Coroner reports showed 125 teenagers died from heroin overdoses in New York City and 140 in California that year. By the late 1970s, teenage heroin abuse subsided and remains low to this day (the teenage heroin toll in 1998: two deaths in New York City, nine in California). Press fear, however, escalated.

1980: The *Washington Post*'s front-page profile (9/28/80) of "Jimmy," a black eight-year-old junkie, ignited pandemonium. Mayor Marion Barry ordered police and teachers to inspect children's arms for needle holes. Despite a $10,000 reward and intensive searches, neither Jimmy nor any other child addict was found. "Jimmy" did not exist, *Post* reporter Janet Cooke later confessed.

1996: Trainspotting panic erupted. In a story that would shame the *National Enquirer*, *USA Today* (7/19/96) declared "smoking or snorting smack is as commonplace as beer for the younger generation." *Rolling Stone* (5/30/96) branded Seattle "junkie town." Citing anecdotes, the article blamed Seattle's tripling in heroin deaths from 1986 to 1994 on "young people" from "white suburban backgrounds." In fact, the Drug Abuse Warning Network (DAWN) reports showed, nearly all of Seattle's increase in heroin fatalities was among aging baby boomers, not kids. The average age of Seattle's 500 heroin decedents from

1995 through 1999 was 40. Only 1 percent were teenagers (*Morbidity and Mortality Weekly Report,* 7/21/00). DAWN reported that, of 2,500 Seattle residents treated for heroin overdoses in 1999, just seven were adolescents.

A Media Chimera

Reporters stampeded to Plano, Texas, spotlighting its 19 teenage and young-adults deaths from heroin overdoses in two years as the tip of a national youth smack epidemic (*L.A. Times,* 11/30/97). As it turned out, the Plano victims didn't know the "chiva" they smoked contained heroin. More crucial, the national media herd never pondered why, if smack was sweeping the young, they had to journey to Plano to find a teen-heroin crisis.

Later, DAWN reports showed 1996's teen-smack panic was another media chimera. Of 8,500 heroin deaths in 1996 and 1997, just 48 were teenagers—and one-fourth of these were Plano's. Of 145,000 hospital treatments for heroin, fewer than 1,000 were youths.

2000: The suburban-teen-heroin hoax resurges, more fraudulent than ever. "Teen heroin use is taking place under their parent's noses," CNN blared (5/9/00, see also identical story 9/21/00). "The drug has moved into the middle-class suburbs with devastating effects."

"Teenagers and young adults are finding the drug more attractive," *ABC News* (7/10/00) declared, blaming the supposed outbreak on the War on Drugs' two favorite scapegoats: suburban teens and minorities. *ABC*'s follow-up concerned Native American heroin abuse in New Mexico (7/12/00).

The simple truth officials and the media refuse to discuss: Today's chief abusers of heroin are not kids or minorities, but white middle-agers. DAWN's latest reports show four-fifths of heroin's overdose-death and hospital cases in 1999 were over age 30. Fewer than 1 percent were teenagers; just 5 percent were under age 25.

Since 1980, the number of Americans imprisoned for drug offenses has soared more than 10-fold, reaching 458,131 in 1997. In California (which now spends $1 billion per year to imprison drug offenders), young adults of color under age 30 are just one-sixth as likely to die from drug abuse, but are twice as likely to be imprisoned for drug offenses, than are white middle-agers (Justice Policy Institute, 8/00, www.cjcj.org/drug).

Why are so few teenagers dying from heroin? They're not using it. The 1999 *National Household Survey on Drug Abuse* reported that of 25,000 12- to 17-year-olds surveyed, just 100 had ever used heroin; only 75 had tried it in the previous year.

Drug-Reform Groups Join In

Both drug-war and drug-reform interests exploit the fiction of a rising teen-drug crisis in order to blame each other for it. [Former drug czar Barry R.] McCaffrey and other drug warriors parade the image that "substance abuse among young people has grown" in their crusade to suppress all "material legitimizing drugs . . . in music, film, television, the Internet and mass market outlets" (*L.A. Times*, 1/2/97).

Groups seeking to reform drug policy counter-claim that "it is the drug war which McCaffrey so ardently supports that is solely responsible for the increase in heroin use among our youth" (*Drug Sense Weekly*, 5/12/00). The reformist Common Sense for Drug Policy (www.csdp.org) even charges that McCaffrey "failed to mention . . . a continuing rise in hard-drug use by our youth," and therefore understated "the dimensions of adolescent drug use"! A CSDP ad campaign, charting the sharp increases in drug imprisonments and overdose deaths from 1980 to 1996, declared, "The more we escalate the drug war, the more young people and others die."

> *"Of 8,500 heroin deaths in 1996 and 1997, just 48 were teenagers."*

The true "dimensions of adolescent drug use" CSDP itself "failed to mention" consist of vanishingly low levels of teenage hard-drug use and casualties, and teenage overdose rates no higher today than in 1980; it's middle-agers who suffer skyrocketing drug demise. Why are reformers silent on this damning reality while helping McCaffrey misrepresent young people as the nation's big drug problem?

"With horrifyingly generic teen-pop acts blaring out from MTV day in and day out, it's a wonder more kids haven't turned to drugs to escape the awful racket," [says *Time* magazine]. The same amen could be applied to the horrifyingly generic racket about "teens and drugs" blaring from Washington, most of the press, and even drug-reform groups that should know better.

There Is No Prescription Drug Abuse Crisis

by Tom Shales

About the author: *Tom Shales is a television critic and editor for the* Washington Post.

TV news doesn't really cover the field of medicine. Instead it goes about the business of fomenting hysteria. Sometimes it's a kind of benign hysteria, the careless spreading of false hope by reporting on some small advance in scientific research that may or may not result in a medical breakthrough three, six, 10 or 20 years down the pike. Don't hold your breath, as the saying goes.

But what the TV news boys and girls really love is a hot juicy story that spreads fear and loathing about drugs and their dangers, real or imagined. Apparently it's good box-office—that is, good for ratings—to air stories that demonize a particular drug and at the same time help to popularize it.

Every network news department has now done a story or two on a drug called OxyContin, a high-powered painkiller prescribed for the most severe cases of suffering; cancer patients are among those most likely to have it prescribed and to consider it a godsend. But it turns out that in some areas where the usual hard-core recreational drugs like crack cocaine are in short supply, substance abusers have found a way to get high on OxyContin. They grind it up into powder and snort it or make it soluble and inject it into their veins.

High on the Story

A national epidemic? No. Not even close. But TV newscasts have tried to portray it that way in stories filled with hype and half-truths. And in the course of "reporting" on abuse of the drug, they've all aired how-to pieces that include handy, easy-to-follow instructions on the correct abuse procedure. They tell you how to get high. Then the correspondents do follow-up reports expressing shock and dismay that the abuse is becoming more popular.

Yeah, more kids are using the drug to get high because they heard about it and even saw how to use it on the evening news.

The hysteria gets whipped up by each succeeding piece until we reach the point, noted in an "NBC Nightly News" report, that some doctors are reluctant to prescribe the drug because it's suddenly got this "bad" reputation. Meanwhile, kids who might never have dreamed of using it to get high are breaking into pharmacies and stealing it or mugging patients as they leave pharmacies after having their legitimate prescriptions filled.

"We are the drug du jour," laments Robin Hogen, executive director of public affairs for Purdue Pharma, the company that makes the drug. For those with intractable pain, with pain that has resisted other medications, OxyContin has been a blessing. But media hysteria threatens that, at least until the panic spotlight moves on to some other medication.

When I was in Los Angeles recently, every TV station was doing stories on Vicodin and how for celebrities it's the drug of choice for recreational use. These reports made Vicodin sound fashionable, cool, chic-irresistible. In the pursuit of ratings, the reporters were encouraging impressionable viewers to get hold of some of that Vicodin and tie one on. You won't just be high, you'll be hip.

Oddly, OxyContin wasn't mentioned. Maybe it will be the drug du jour in Los Angeles when the Vicodin stories start falling flat.

TV reporters have been "hysterical from Day One," Hogen says, in reporting on abuses of OxyContin and on deaths allegedly caused by overdoses. Well, not "caused by." The reporters are careful. They usually say "linked to." Even that may be a stretch of the facts. It's been repeatedly reported that the drug can be linked to 59 deaths in Kentucky within a recent year. Why Kentucky, of all places? That's part of the story the reporters usually leave out.

Even ignoring that, the figure may very well be bogus. Once one reporter uses it, all other reporters feel free to use it without double-checking. But there is no hard evidence that OxyContin played a key role in 59 Kentuckians keeling over. David Jones, an official with the Kentucky State Medical Examiner's office, looked into the claim and wrote a letter to Purdue Pharma: "I am unaware of any reliable data in Kentucky that proves OxyContin

> *"Stories that demonize a particular drug . . . help to popularize it."*

is causing a lot of deaths. In the State M.E. Office, we are seeing an increase in the number of deaths from ingesting several different prescription drugs and mixing them with alcohol. OxyContin is sometimes one of these drugs."

From Local to National

What's happened, Hogen says, is that a regional story has been inflated into a national one by TV journalists. He says abuse of OxyContin is confined mainly to "rural pockets" in five states: Maine, West Virginia, Virginia, Alabama and Kentucky. Why rural areas of those states? "Because the people who abuse drugs there can't get heroin or crack cocaine the way people in big cities can," Hogen says. "It's part of the economics of the drug business. The abuse is mainly in poor rural communities where there is high unemployment and high substance abuse already."

> *"A national [prescription drug abuse] epidemic? No. Not even close."*

As the TV reporters have made vividly clear, manipulating the drug by crushing it (thus bypassing a time-release feature) and then injecting it can give a sudden and drastically euphoric high. They usually trot out an abuser to describe how delicious and wonderful the high can be, thus making it sound still more enticing to what we might call the Drug Abuse Community.

But there is also in America something called a Pain Community. These are people suffering intensely from pain or involved in research to find more and better ways to control it. OxyContin gives effective pain relief for 12 hours with no euphoria involved, Hogen says, but TV news is giving it a reputation as a cheap kick for drug-crazed thrill-seekers.

Who Needs the Facts?

Could the network news departments turn a regional problem into a national problem by continuing with these alarmist reports? "Absolutely," Hogen says. "None of these clowns on television are reporting the beneficial aspects of the drug. Only the abuse. They are scaring pharmacists, scaring doctors and scaring patients."

Contrary to reports, the drug is not new but was introduced in 1995. Finding a way to abuse it has been a fairly recent occurrence, apparently. Hogen says stories about the abuse just happened to break during the first week of the February 2001 Sweeps. What luck for TV newscasters. "They jumped on it as if they had discovered gold," he says. Each network in turn dutifully did its report, with each reporter trying to top the previous guy's piece by making the drug sound deadlier, the high sound higher, the hazards more hazardous.

It isn't hard to imagine news directors at local stations throughout the country now wondering aloud at staff meetings why the station hasn't had its own report on the big OxyContin scare. You can't just let a nice panicky rabble-rouser like that slip through your fingers. Then more kids and other substance abusers get exposed to the story and the drug leaps forward in popularity and infamy.

There is, apparently, no epidemic of OxyContin abuse. And while movie stars may currently favor Vicodin as their high of choice, there's no epidemic of Vicodin abuse either.

What's epidemic is bad journalism. But you won't see Dan Rather or Tom Brokaw or Peter Jennings doing any stories on that.

Chapter 3

Are Drug Treatment and Prevention Programs Effective?

Chapter Preface

Drug Abuse Resistance Education (DARE) is the most widely taught drug education program in the United States. For seventeen weeks each academic year, specially trained uniformed police officers give children in the fifth and sixth grades lessons in drug education. They reinforce the curriculum with their professional knowledge of the harms of drug abuse. At a cost of $220 million a year, 75 percent of the nation's school districts use DARE to teach children how to deal with the pressures to use illegal drugs they may experience during adolescence.

Numerous critics claim that the DARE program is ineffective. For example, some studies have indicated that although DARE may have an immediate effect on children, it has not proven to influence their likeliness to use drugs when they grow older. Others contend that DARE may have unintended effects on children's attitudes towards drugs. While enrolled in a DARE program, a student said, "I don't think DARE works. It sounds weird, but in a way it kind of makes you want to try drugs, to see what they're like. . . . I guess DARE makes you curious."

Amid these claims, Greg Levant, president and founding director of DARE, defends the drug education program. In response to the studies indicating that DARE has no lasting effect on youths' attitudes toward drugs, Levant argues that "while there are still 23 million drug users in this country today, their average age is rising, indicating that prevention programs are having positive results on young people." In addition, Levant claims, a national Gallup survey of DARE alumni revealed that 90 percent felt that drug education helped them to avoid drugs and alcohol and regarded drug use as dangerous.

In the following chapter, the authors evaluate the effectiveness of various anti-drug programs and other approaches used in reducing drug abuse.

Drug Addiction Treatment Is Effective

by Alan I. Leshner

About the author: *Alan I. Leshner is director of the National Institute on Drug Abuse (NIDA), a federal program that conducts research in an attempt to improve drug abuse and addiction prevention, treatment, and policy.*

More than 4 million Americans are addicted to drugs, and fewer than half of them have received any treatment. Many of the remaining millions have actively sought treatment but have been turned away for lack of programs and resources. The consequence of this severe nationwide shortfall in resources is unnecessary devastation for the addicts, their families, employers, and communities.

Consider these facts:

- Lost work-force productivity due to drug abuse costs the nation at least $14 billion annually, including losses due to unemployment, impairment, absenteeism, and premature deaths. On the other hand, research shows that treatment increases the likelihood of employment by 40 percent or more.
- Crime related to drug addiction costs the nation an estimated $57 billion per year, not including victims' and law officers' medical costs. However, research has shown that addicts who undergo treatment are 40 percent less likely to be arrested for violent or nonviolent crimes.
- Addicts who receive appropriate treatment in prison are 50 to 60 percent less likely to be arrested again during the 18 months following their release. According to several conservative estimates, every $1 invested in addiction treatment yields a return of $4 to $7 in reduced crime and criminal justice costs.
- Drug abuse treatment reduces injection drug users' risk of spreading HIV and other infections by as much as 60 percent, and abstaining addicts do not need costly emergency room treatment for overdoses.

The Underlying Problems

Making high-quality drug addiction treatment widely available can alleviate much of the devastation caused by drugs in the United States. However, treat-

From "The Sense in Saving Drug Addicts," by Alan I. Leshner, *Boston Globe*, September 5, 1999.

ment receives relatively little support from the public. Why? The underlying problems are a lack of understanding of the true nature of drug addiction and failure to recognize the effectiveness of its treatment.

The prevailing perception is that drug addiction is simply willful and defiant antisocial behavior. This leads to the attitude that addicts do not deserve help. And if a treated addict relapses to drug use, the fall is attributed to bad character.

These might have been defensible points of view 30 years ago, based on what was then known about addiction. However, modern science has since shown them to be completely off the mark.

Most untreated addicts cannot resist abusing drugs, even in the face of severe negative health and social consequences. This compulsion comes about because prolonged drug use causes structural and functional changes in the brain. With modern brain-imaging techniques, scientists actually can see these dramatic alterations in brain function.

Vulnerability and Choice

For some people, the fact that voluntary drug abuse precedes addiction means that addicts do not deserve treatment. This same logic would suggest that we should not offer treatment to people with many other chronic diseases, almost all of which involve a combination of vulnerability and choice. In hypertension, for example, there is an underlying vulnerability, but the impact of the disease depends on diet, exercise, and whether one chooses to work at a stressful job.

This does not mean drug addicts should be absolved of responsibility for their actions. On the contrary, the addict must actively participate and comply with treatment regimens if the outcome is to be successful.

Many treated addicts relapse, but it is wrong to conclude that treatment has failed, or that the addict is incorrigible. Most addicts, like most patients with asthma or hypertension, gain control over their disease gradually, often over the course of many treatment episodes. Drug abuse treatment should be judged by the same criteria used for other chronic disease interventions: Will it help lengthen the time between relapses, ensure that the individual can function fully in society, and minimize long-term damage to the body?

Making Treatment Better

A variety of studies from the National Institutes of Health, Columbia University, the University of Pennsylvania, and other institutions have all shown that drug treatment reduces use by 50 to 60 percent. This success rate is not ideal, but it is comparable to—or better than—the results of treatments for many other chronic diseases including diabetes, hypertension, cancer, depression, and heart disease.

Moreover, medical research is making addiction treatment better all the time. Science is equipping treatment providers with more and better tools to tailor treatment to individual patients' needs, as determined by his or her choice of drug (or drugs), the addiction history, as well as concurrent diagnoses, such as HIV/AIDS or depression, and environmental factors.

The conclusion is inescapable. As much as one might deplore the addict's initial decision to take drugs, it is clearly in everyone's interest that we rise above our moral outrage and offer treatment to all who need it.

A variety of recent proposals suggest that the country may at last be ready to abandon discredited, self-defeating ideas about drug addiction. These proposals would increase financing for more treatment slots, expand the breadth and usefulness of treatment research, equalize health insurance coverage for drug addiction treatment when compared with other medical treatments, and expand treatment for addicts involved in the criminal justice system.

The sooner these proposals move forward, the sooner the national nightmare of drug addiction will abate.

Methadone Treatment Is an Effective Treatment for Heroin Addiction

by James Cooper

About the author: *James Cooper is associate director for medical affairs in the Division of Clinical and Services Research at the National Institute on Drug Abuse (NIDA), a federal program that conducts research in an attempt to improve drug abuse and addiction prevention, treatment, and policy.*

In the United States, approximately 600,000 people are addicted to heroin. In recent years, data from several sources suggest that there is an increase in new heroin users as well as an emerging pattern of drug use among the young. Heroin addiction is often associated with increased criminal activity and human suffering. Since 1988, there has been a dramatic increase in the prevalence of human immunodeficiency virus (HIV), hepatitis C virus (HCV), and tuberculosis among intravenous heroin users. From 1991 to 1995 in major metropolitan areas, the annual number of heroin-related emergency room visits has increased from 36,000 to 76,000, and the annual number of heroin-related deaths has increased from 2,300 to 4,000. The associated morbidity and mortality further underscore the enormous human, economic, and societal costs of heroin addiction.

Over the last 25 years, a significant body of evidence has accumulated on the etiology of heroin addiction and the safety and effectiveness of one of the treatments most often used for heroin addiction—methadone. Methadone treatment has been evaluated more rigorously than any other drug abuse treatment modality, resulting in voluminous data, much of which has been published either by NIDA or its grantees. . . .

A Chronic Relapsing Disease

Twenty-five years of research on addiction has provided the scientific evidence to define addiction as a chronic relapsing disease of the brain. In the case

Excerpted from James Cooper's presentation on methadone to the joint New York State Assembly Committee on Alcoholism and Drug Abuse and Committee on Health Hearings, December 11, 1998.

of heroin, addiction results from the prolonged effects of heroin on the brain. Reward pathways located in the mesolimbic area of the brain are activated by opiates such as heroin, as well as by other addictive drugs. These pathways appear to be a common element in what keeps drug users taking heroin and other drugs of abuse. All addictive drugs, including heroin, nicotine, cocaine or amphetamines appear to affect this circuit. Prolonged opiate use causes pervasive changes in brain function that persist long after the individual stops taking the drug. Brain imaging and other modern technologies show that the addicted brain is distinctly different from the non-addictive brain, manifested by changes in brain metabolic activity, receptor availability, gene expression, and responsiveness to environmental cues. Understanding that addiction is, at its core, a consequence of fundamental changes in brain function means that a goal of treatment must be either to reverse or compensate for those brain changes. This can be accomplished with medications or behavioral treatments, or by a combination of the two. This is basically what is accomplished through the use of medications such as methadone and LAAM [levo-alpha acetyl-methadol, a medication for heroin addiction] when they are used alone or combined with behavioral and social treatments—they can help to reverse or compensate for the brain changes that occurred during the addiction process.

It is this thorough understanding of the neurobiological basis of addiction that led a recent NIH Consensus Development Panel to conclude that addiction is in fact a medical disorder.

> *"Understanding the biological basis of addiction helps in understanding the efficacy of methadone treatment."*

That conclusion was reached after a November 1997, Consensus Development Conference on the Effective Medical Treatment of Heroin Addiction. This forum provided NIH with an independent review and analysis by non-government scientists of the current research knowledge base on heroin addiction and its treatment and its relationship to the current status of the delivery of treatment services. The panel of experts was specifically asked to review the scientific evidence to support conceptualization of opiate dependence as a medical disorder. They unanimously concluded that careful study of the natural history and thorough research at the genetic, molecular, neuronal, and epidemiological levels has proven that opiate addiction is a medical disorder. . . .

The Efficacy of Methadone

Understanding the biological basis of addiction helps in understanding the efficacy of methadone treatment. It also helps to understand why medications cannot be terminated prematurely, especially when one considers how easy it is for many people to relapse to drug use. Just like diabetes and many other medical disorders, addiction is chronic and relapsing. It is imperative that treatments be administered properly to reduce the chances that the addicted individual will relapse.

We have learned much from the many large NIDA funded methadone treatment evaluation studies over the last 25 years. Methadone has been found to be a highly effective treatment for heroin addiction. There are, however, still many misconceptions about what methadone is and what it is not. This medication occupies the same opioid (endorphin) receptors as heroin, but pharmacologically it is quite different. For example, each time heroin is

> *"Methadone has been found to be a highly effective treatment for heroin addiction."*

used, there is an almost immediate "rush" or brief period of euphoria, which wears off relatively quickly, resulting in a "crash" and craving to use more heroin. In contrast, methadone and LAAM have a more gradual onset of action when administered orally; there is no rush. Research has demonstrated that, when methadone is given in regular doses by a physician, it has the ability to block the euphoria caused by heroin, if the individual does try to take heroin.

Studies have consistently shown that methadone is highly effective in retaining in treatment a large proportion of patients, reducing their intravenous drug use and criminal activity and enhancing their social productivity. In addition, research has shown that methadone is not only effective in treating heroin addiction, but it is cost-effective as well, especially when one compares it to the cost of incarceration.

A Part of the Program

From a public health perspective, methadone treatment is better than other treatment modalities in retaining patients who enter treatment for heroin addiction. Retention rates are dose dependent and are further enhanced when psychosocial interventions are made available by qualified professional therapists. Enhanced retention rates are critical when one considers the abundance of research which demonstrates that the longer a patient stays in treatment, the more likely he/she will stop or at least significantly reduce drug use during and after treatment. These findings alone are important during these times of increasing heroin availability and HIV and hepatitis infection among drug users and their sexual partners. Numerous studies have shown that drug abuse treatment, especially methadone programs, are highly effective in preventing the spread of HIV. Individuals who enter drug treatment programs reduce their drug use, which in turn leads to fewer instances of drug-related HIV risk behaviors such as needle sharing and unsafe sex practices. . . .

My remarks about what the science has taught us to date about methadone treatment effectiveness do however need some qualification. Methadone treatment is effective when methadone is part of what I would consider a quality treatment program. In this type of program, a well-trained treatment physician will provide patients with adequate methadone doses to reduce not only the individual's opiate use, but their craving as well. Ensuring the patient gets an appropriate dose of methadone will increase the likelihood of both the patient's retention and treatment outcome. Furthermore, outcomes are improved when programs allow patients to stay in treatment long enough to ensure that rehabilitation has been complete and that the risk of relapse is minimal. Simply put, good programs will individualize treatment to meet the needs of a particular patient. Just as a physician treating any other illness would do, patients need to be evaluated on a patient-by-patient basis. Some may only need to be treated for a short time, while others may require a longer treatment regimen.

Equally important, treatment programs must address the whole person. Meaning, they make available when necessary a variety of psychosocial and vocational rehabilitation opportunities to help the patient become a functional member of society. A quality program will also address all aspects of the patient's addiction, including any co-morbid mental or medical disorders that the patient may have. They do this by providing appropriate pharmacological, psychological or behavioral interventions to treat disorders in addition to the patient's addiction and insure that patients receive AIDS risk reduction counseling and medical care as needed.

Availability of Treatment

There is increasing concern among the field about the availability of treatment to those in need. The majority of my following comments on this aspect of treatment are based on findings from the statement issued by the NIH Consensus Development Panel.

The Panel raised concern about the current limited availability of methadone and LAAM treatment for the approximate 600,000 people known to be addicted to heroin. "Most do not receive treatment, and the financial cost of untreated heroin addiction to the individual, the family, and to society is estimated to be approximately $20 billion per year." The Panel stressed the importance of providing more comprehensive services, such as substance abuse counseling, psychosocial therapy and other supportive services to enhance retention and to achieve even more successful outcomes. Equally important, they identified a number of barriers to the effective use of methadone treatment related to misperception and stigma attached to heroin addiction, the people who are addicted, those who treat them, and the settings in which services are provided. Thus, the Panel urged that methadone and LAAM be made more widely available and that the current barriers be removed.

"When methadone is given in regular doses by a physician, it has the ability to block the euphoria caused by heroin."

To meet these objectives, the Panel made a number of specific recommendations. For example, they strongly recommended that legislators and regulators recognize that methadone maintenance treatment is both cost-effective and compassionate and that benefits for treatment be part of public and private in-surance programs. . . .

Strong Science

In conclusion, I would like to reiterate that 25 years of research has shown that drug addiction treatment, especially methadone, is quite effective in reducing not only drug use but also in reducing the spread of infections like HIV/AIDS and in decreasing criminal behavior. Thus, drug treatment benefits not only the individual patient but also both public health and public safety.

We have come a great distance in our approaches to understanding and treating drug addiction, but we still have quite a distance ahead of us. We can improve the quality and availability of treatment in the country if we put treating addiction on equal footing with other chronic diseases. The science in this field is strong and the success rates for treating addiction are comparable to or better than those for many other illnesses. Expanding access to treatments will benefit us all.

Antidrug Media Campaigns Reduce Drug Abuse

by Lloyd D. Johnston

About the author: *Lloyd D. Johnston is a research scientist at the Institute for Social Research at the University of Michigan.*

Under a series of investigator-initiated, competing research grants from the National Institute on Drug Abuse, which funds Monitoring the Future, my colleagues and I have conducted an annual national survey of 12th grade students in the coterminous United States each year since 1975. Starting in 1991 we have also surveyed nationally representative samples of 8th graders and 10th graders annually, with the result that some 50,000 students located in approximately 420 secondary schools now participate in the survey each year.

Among the subjects we track that are of most relevance are: (1) students' use of a wide range of drugs, (2) their disapproval of the use of these drugs, (3) their beliefs about the harmfulness of these drugs, (4) their recalled levels of exposure to anti-drug advertising, (5) their judgements about the creditability of the ads, and (6) their judgements of the amount of impact their exposure to the ad campaigns has had on their own use of drugs. The questions dealing with media campaigns go back to 1987, when the Partnership for a Drug Free America (PDFA) campaign began, while the measures of drug use, related attitudes, and beliefs go back to 1976.

The Importance of Attitudes and Beliefs

First, let me say that I think that well-planned and well-executed media campaigns are very important, because of their capacity to influence young people's attitudes and beliefs about drugs. One of the most important findings to emerge from Monitoring the Future over the past quarter of a century is the strong negative association between the amount of danger young people associate with a

Excerpted from Lloyd D. Johnston's testimony before the United States House of Representatives, House Committee on Government Reform, Subcommittee on Criminal Justice, Drug Policy, and Human Resources, October 14, 1999.

given drug (which we have called "perceived risk") and their use of that drug. Another is the strong negative association between personal disapproval of using a drug and the use of that drug.

When the perceived risk of using marijuana increased substantially among American adolescents over the twelve-year period 1979–1991, their use of marijuana fell steadily. Then, a year later, as perceived risk for marijuana reversed course in 1992 and began to fall, use followed and began to rise in 1993. (Note that in this case perceived risk was a leading indicator of change in use.)

Personal disapproval of using a drug—which in the aggregate translates into peer disapproval—shows a similar inverse association over time with usage levels, though not in this case as a leading indicator. We believe that both perceived risk and peer disapproval are very important determinants of use, and that perceived risk operates partly through its effect on peer disapproval by influencing norms against use. Put more simply, if a drug comes to be seen as more dangerous, then its use is likely to be more disapproved within the peer group.

In a series of journal articles specifically on this subject, we have shown that these powerful cross-time associations cannot be explained away by concurrent shifts in a number of other lifestyle factors. Disapproval and perceived risk remain powerful predictors of use, even when controlling for a host of other known risk factors. These articles also demonstrate that these attitudes are more able to explain the changes in use, than use is able to explain the changes in attitudes. . . .

Disapproval and Decline

By 1996 the media frenzy over crack had reached its peak, public response was sizeable, and a young first-round draft pick for the NBA named Len Bias died from cocaine use. (As it happened, the media initially reported Len Bias's death as resulting from his first exposure to cocaine—a conclusion which was later contradicted—but that was the story that young people heard.) The proportion of young people who saw cocaine use (even experimental use) as dangerous soared, disapproval increased, and usage levels began a long and quite dramatic decline.

I think there are two overarching conclusions, which can be drawn from these data on marijuana and cocaine. One is that the levels of drug use among young people can be changed quite substantially—indeed,

> *"Well-planned and well-executed media campaigns are very important, because of their capacity to influence young people's attitudes and beliefs about drugs."*

they already have been. Second, attitudes and beliefs appear to have played a major role in bringing about the changes observed. . . .

Of course, changes in drug use are not always in the direction we would prefer. After an 11-year decline in marijuana use and a shorter, 6-year decline in cocaine use, the trend lines for both began to rise in the 1990's. Again, attitudes and beliefs played major roles. As we have written elsewhere, we think that multiple forces converged and led to a weakening of anti-drug attitudes. One very important development was that media news coverage of the drug issue fell off the national screen during the build-up to the Gulf War in 1991, and it did not reappear until several years later, as journalists became aware that the drug problem was re-emerging among a newer generation of youth. Second, and also media-related, the nation's electronic and print media cut back considerably in both the quantity and quality of the time and space they contributed pro bono for the placement of the anti-drug ads produced by the Partnership for a Drug-Free America. In other words, the ad campaign became less visible to young people, as I will substantiate below.

Generational Forgetting

Interestingly, the resurgence of drug use in the nineties was specific to adolescents. . . . We take this to mean that a newer generation of young people was growing up not knowing as much about the dangers of drugs. We believe this was partly due to the fact that they were witnessing less use among their friends (and also among public figures) than did their predecessors, because drug use rates had declined so much. But, it was also partly due to the fact that they were being exposed to many fewer messages about the dangers of drugs in the media, either through the airing of the anti-drug commercials or through news stories.

> *"Unless we institutionalize some of the mechanisms for educating children about the consequences of drug use . . . future naive generations are very likely to relapse into use."*

We have labeled this phenomenon "generational forgetting"—the loss of knowledge by the country's youth of the dangers of drugs through the process of generational replacement. Its implications for social policy are considerable. It suggests that, unless we institutionalize some of the mechanisms for educating children about the consequences of drug use and provide them persuasive reasons not to use, future naive generations are very likely to relapse into use. In fact, as the resurgence of drug use in the early nineties illustrates, the danger of society's taking its eye off the ball may be greatest right after a period of decline in use, when complacency can set in. We never can permanently win the so-called "war on drugs": the best we can do is to win the battle for each generation as they grow up.

The relevance to anti-drug advertising campaigns is this. Such campaigns constitute one of the few means by which we can institutionalize the education and socialization of youngsters with regard to drugs. It also allows parents to be reminded of their important roles in prevention. We cannot get the media to keep paying attention to the problem if they do not wish to, or they think it not newsworthy. And we have not been particularly successful at influencing the portrayals of drug use young people see in entertainment programming or in the behavior of public role models—both very likely important influences on young people. That leaves two primary avenues which as a society we can utilize to reach youngsters—the schools and paid media. I think we should be using both very actively.

Youth Reactions

That said, I would be the first to agree that how a media campaign (or school-based prevention program) is carried out can make a world of difference. Effective persuasion, particularly of today's media-savvy young people, is a formidable task. Academics like myself may be able to come up with valid strategies and approaches, but then there is a creative leap that must be made successfully in order to yield an effective finished message. That, I firmly believe, is the domain of the creative professionals who do this kind of work for a living.

As you well know, the federally backed partnership—between the Office of National Drug Control Policy (ONDCP) and the private sector Partnership for a Drug Free America (PDFA)—builds heavily upon the previous ten to twelve years of work of the PDFA. As the PDFA's campaign started to get underway in 1987, we added a set of questions to our ongoing surveys of American high school seniors to determine their degree of exposure to the campaign ads, as well as their opinions about them. (The same questions were added to the surveys of the younger students when we began to survey them in 1991.) While these questions do not ask specifically about the PDFA campaign, that campaign has accounted for the preponderance of the anti-drug advertising since then, which leads us to interpret the students' answers as predominantly in response to that campaign.

I would like to share with you some of what we have learned from tracking these questions over succeeding 8th, 10th, and 12th grade classes. First, . . . levels of media support (in millions of dollars of value, as estimated by the Partnership) changed over time, and the level of perceived risk 12th graders associated with marijuana use, changed along with those expenditure levels. Let me be clear, I do not take these results by themselves as proof of a causal association, nor do I think that advertising was the only important influence changing over this time interval that might have contributed to the changes in perceived risk or actual drug use

> *"[Anti-drug campaigns] allows parents to be reminded of their important roles in prevention."*

(as I have just discussed). Nevertheless, there is some association here which certainly would be consistent with a causal connection. Note particularly . . . the considerable decline, from $365 million to $220 million, in the estimated annual value of the media-contributed time and space between 1991 and 1997.

During that same time interval, the proportion of students reporting weekly or daily exposure to the ads also declined steadily, consistent with the decline in the PDFA advertising contributions. In 1998 the estimated market value of the ad coverage began to rise again, as the federal effort began to kick in. . . .

As youth exposure to the anti-drug ad campaign declined through most of the nineties, so did the judged effect of the ads on student drug-taking behaviors and related attitudes. In the early nineties, when the campaign was at its peak levels, very high proportions of our respondents said that the anti-drug ads they saw had caused them to have less favorable attitudes toward drugs, and decreased their likelihood of using drugs. Among 8th graders surveyed in 1991, over 80% said that the ads had reduced their own likelihood of using drugs at least "to a little extent," over 70% said it had influenced them "to some extent," and over 50% said it actually had influenced them to a "great or very great extent." I have always found these numbers to be very impressive, considering the fact that teenagers generally do not like to admit that anyone is influencing them, particularly anyone who is trying to influence them. But, as the frequency of ad placement waned over the next six or seven years, so did students' reports of how much effect the campaign was having on them, as logically would be expected if their answers were truthful.

> *"As the frequency of [anti-drug] ad placement waned . . . so did students' reports of how much effect the campaign was having on them."*

One final point about the reaction of young people to the ad material used in the campaign. We have always felt that for such ad campaigns to be successful, retaining credibility with the target audience is essential. To measure credibility, we ask a question about the extent to which the respondent thinks the ads, taken collectively, overstate the dangers or risks of drug use. In general, it turns out that the judged credibility of the ads has been rather good and fairly stable over time, with only around 20% of the 10th and 12th graders saying that the dangers of drugs were overstated "a lot." For the 8th graders, a somewhat higher proportion says the same—around 35–38%.

A Strategic Point of View

To summarize, the attitudes and beliefs of youth that the anti-drug media campaigns seek to influence have been demonstrated to be among the most important determinants of drug use. When a high rate of coverage of the ads can be attained, as the new federal effort seeks to accomplish and as the PDFA campaign was able to attain in the early nineties, adolescents' exposure can be raised to quite high rates. More importantly, adolescents' judgements of the impact of the ads on their own drug-using propensity and their drug-related attitudes can be impressively high when the exposure rate is high. And, the campaigns so far seem to have retained a relatively high and consistent level of credibility with the youth target audiences. These findings should bolster our belief that a well-run and sustained advertising campaign can make an important difference.

From a strategic point of view, it is important to realize that intentional use of the media represents one of the very few channels available through which we can institutionalize the education and socialization of youth with regard to drugs. (Prevention efforts in the school represent the primary other such channel.) In the absence of institutionalizing such efforts, we risk the continued reemergence of drug epidemics among our young people. The lessons learned from the casualties occurring in any one epidemic will be "forgotten," as a newer and more naive generation grows up and replaces the generation which experienced the epidemic firsthand. Such "generational forgetting" will occur repeatedly in the absence of vigorous societal efforts to prevent it. The National Youth Anti-drug Media Campaign represents one of the most promising such efforts.

Needle-Exchange Programs Reduce the Harms of Intravenous Drug Use

by Jon Fuller

About the author: *Jon Fuller is assistant director of the Adult Clinical AIDS Program at Boston Medical Center, associate professor of medicine at Boston University's School of Medicine, and a Jesuit priest.*

In a remarkable rejection of scientific data and its own experts' opinions, the Clinton Administration announced in April 1998 its long-awaited decision regarding the expiring ban on Federal support of needle-exchange programs (N.E.P.'s).

The Administration's logic was not immediately obvious. While it recognized that N.E.P.'s reduce H.I.V. transmission and do not increase drug use, it refused to lift the ban but encouraged local governments to use their own resources to fund exchange programs. Since the Administration's stated reason was its concern that lifting the ban might send the wrong message to children, it is not evident why the states are being encouraged to do what the Federal Government should not.

In his reaction to the decision, R. Scott Hitt, an AIDS physician and chairman of the President's Advisory Council on H.I.V.-AIDS, was quoted in *The New York Times* as saying that "at best this is hypocrisy, at worst, it's a lie. And no matter what, it's immoral."

The Failure to Save Lives

As a church we need to consider carefully Dr. Hitt's evaluation, for it reminds us that a fundamental moral issue is at stake: the failure to act to save human lives. Dr. Hitt's criticism can as appropriately be directed toward the churches as toward the Administration: We can seem to be more concerned about potential "scandal" (sending the wrong message about drug use) than with N.E.P.'s ability to prevent lethal H.I.V. transmissions to particularly vulnerable populations.

Our silence or negative attitudes toward N.E.P.'s are puzzling, since the Catholic tradition is particularly well suited for responding to complicated questions such as needle exchange. We have nuanced tools for judging complex moral cases, we have a long tradition of engagement with the forces of society that particularly impinge on the poor and marginated, and we are in a unique position to provide moral leadership on this complex public issue that so confuses and frightens people.

> *"Our silence or negative attitudes toward needle exchange programs (N.E.P.'s) are puzzling."*

Here I will review briefly the history and merits of needle-exchange programs from a public health perspective, and then demonstrate how, using traditional Catholic moral principles, we may not only tolerate but may even cooperate with these programs. Our particular responsibility to protect the lives of those without voice or power, those trapped in the cycle of addiction and those at risk for being infected should urge us to take a leadership role in the development of public policy on this life-threatening issue.

International Experience

Based on the assessment that it is impossible to eliminate completely intravenous drug use in society, needle exchanges were first instituted in Amsterdam in 1983 to prevent the transmission of hepatitis B and H.I.V. (human immunodeficiency virus, the causative agent of AIDS), which can occur when needles are shared. While recovery from addiction was still sought as a long-term goal, N.E.P.'s were designed to protect addicts from these viruses in the meantime, and also to prevent secondary transmission to sexual partners and—in the case of pregnant women—transmission to developing infants. Needle exchanges have since been credited with a decrease in the number of new H.I.V. infections occurring among drug users in many cities around the globe. Indeed, three Catholic agencies sponsor needle exchanges in Australia. According to David Waterford of the Adelaide Diocesan AIDS Council, Southern Australia (with 55 exchange programs for a population of 1.2 million) has reported no new H.I.V. infections resulting from needle sharing from 1995 through 1998.

The U.S. Experience

In striking contrast to the decline in H.I.V. infections among addicts in these other countries, the United States has seen injection drug use increase as the source of H.I.V. infection among new AIDS cases from approximately 1 percent in 1981 to 31 percent of cases documented in 1997. When transmission from injectors to sexual partners and to infants is also included, 40 percent of new cases may be attributed to drug use. Three-fourths of H.I.V. transmissions to women and children have come from drug injectors, and among injectors who have been diagnosed with AIDS, 77 percent of women and 79 percent of men have come from communities of color.

Because of this increasing threat posed by needle transmissions, more than 100 needle exchanges have now been established in the United States. Many were begun as "guerrilla" activities by addicts in recovery who understood the realities of addiction and the potential harm of needle sharing.

However, as opposed to their fairly widespread acceptance in many other countries, needle-exchange programs encountered considerable resistance in the United States when they were first proposed. Neighborhoods voiced concerns about property values, security and the possibility that discarded needles might be left where children could play with them. Some objected that bringing needles into minority neighborhoods was a genocidal act, demonstrating an indifference to the particularly heavy burden of addiction already being borne by these communities. Despite a 1991 U.S. Government Accounting Office study that concluded that needle-exchange programs "hold some promise as an AIDS prevention strategy," Congress passed legislation in 1992 prohibiting the use of Federal funds to support needle-exchange programs until the Surgeon General could certify that they did not encourage drug use and were effective in reducing the spread of H.I.V.

Exchange—Not Distribution

The vast majority of U.S. N.E.P.'s are designed to be needle exchange, not needle distribution services—providing a clean needle and syringe only in exchange for a used set. In contrast with vending machines that dispense syringes in some European cities, U.S. programs consider human contact a critical aspect of the exchange, with education and referrals to health care and recovery programs being offered at every encounter. The human contact and protection from disease that these programs offer communicates a powerful message to addicts that their lives and well-being are still valued by the community, even though they may not yet be able to break the cycle of addictive behavior.

In their 1989 pastoral letter on the AIDS epidemic, "Called to Compassion and Responsibility," the U.S. bishops raised serious concerns about needle-exchange programs as a means of limiting the spread of H.I.V. The

"Needle exchanges have . . . been credited with a decrease in the number of new H.I.V. infections occurring among drug users."

bishops questioned whether these programs might increase drug use instead of reducing H.I.V. transmission and whether supporting them might send the wrong message by appearing to condone or even to make drug use easier. Although a significant scientific literature has developed in support of exchange programs since that letter was written, there has been little further public discussion of needle exchange within the church, and almost no attention has been given to this issue in the ethical and theological literature. Several state bishops' confer-ences have spoken against exchange programs, but to my knowledge the only U.S. Catholic agency that has actively promoted N.E.P.'s is the Catholic Family Center in the Diocese of Rochester, N.Y.

Scientific Evaluation of Exchange Programs

Numerous studies of the risks and benefits of needle exchange have now been published, and in 1995 an advisory panel of the National Research Council and the Institute of Medicine was constituted to review the state of the question. The group observed that, although existing drug paraphernalia laws were intended to decrease drug use, by inhibiting users from possessing needles "they unwit-tingly contribute to the sharing of contaminated ones. While the act of giving a needle to an injection drug user has a powerful symbolism that has sparked fears about the potential negative effects of needle-exchange programs, there is no credible evidence that drug use is increased among participants or that it increases the number of new initiates to injection drug use."

> *"The United States has seen injection drug use increase as the source of H.I.V. infection among new AIDS cases."*

After observing that public support for these programs tends to increase over time, the panel concluded that "well-implemented needle-exchange programs can be effective in preventing the spread of H.I.V. and do not increase the use of illegal drugs. We therefore recommend that the Surgeon General make the de-termination necessary to rescind the present prohibition against applying any Federal funds to support needle exchange programs."

In February 1997 a consensus panel of the National Institutes of Health indi-cated that these programs "show reduction in risk behavior as high as 80 per-cent in injecting drug users, with estimates of a 30 percent reduction of H.I.V." The panel therefore "strongly recommended the lifting of government restric-tions on needle-exchange programs and the legalization of pharmacy sales of sterile injecting equipment."

In March 1998 the President's AIDS Council also urged that the ban be lifted, noting that every day 33 Americans are infected from dirty needles. Other en-dorsements of needle exchange have come from numerous groups concerned with the common good and the public health, including the American Medical Association, the American Public Health Association, the American Bar Asso-ciation and the National Conference of Mayors. As increasing dialogue has oc-curred between operators of needle exchanges and public health and law en-forcement agencies, some previously illegal operations have now become officially sponsored or at least tolerated.

While the consensus of scientific and public health opinion supports needle exchanges as providing significant benefits without causing harm, how do we analyze these programs from a moral perspective? Some judge that we must oppose them lest we be seen as condoning behavior judged to be gravely wrong, while others propose that we tolerate them by not opposing their being conducted by others. A third perspective, which can be justified by traditional moral principles, holds that the potential harm of needle sharing is so great that our commitment to the preservation of life and to caring for the most vulnerable members of society urges us to take the lead in supporting these programs.

Our tradition has long recognized that in a complex world we are frequently faced with the prospect of cooperating to some degree with individuals or groups whose goals we may not fully share. The "principle of cooperation" assists us in adjudicating a wide variety of questions, ranging from paying taxes to a government whose activities are not always condoned, to cooperating in an indirect manner with an illicit medical procedure. Although an extensive analysis of the principle and its application is not possible here, for the sake of discussion I propose to describe briefly how cooperation with N.E.P.'s can satisfy the principle's six criteria. (At the risk of employing a few unfamiliar phrases, the technical language traditionally used when invoking the principle has been included in this discussion.)

The Requirements

The first requirement—that the object of our action be good or morally neutral—is satisfied by the fact that simply exchanging a dirty needle for a sterile one is itself morally indifferent.

In the second test we must consider if our cooperation would be intending or promoting illicit activity. Since N.E.P.'s do not encourage or condone drug use—but only attempt to make drug use less harmful—our cooperation would be material and therefore permitted, whereas formal cooperation (explicit support or encouragement of drug use) would not.

The third criterion requires that the illicit activity (in this case, injection of a drug) not be the same as the action in which we are cooperating (exchange of needles). In the principle's technical language, cooperation with needle exchange would be judged as mediate (permitted) rather than immediate (forbidden).

"The vast majority of U.S. N.E.P.'s are designed to be needle exchange, not needle distribution services."

In the fourth test our action must be distanced from the illicit act as much as possible. Since we would be cooperating with needle exchange rather than with drug injection, N.E.P.'s meet the test that our cooperation be remote, not proximate.

The fifth criterion—that cooperation be justified by a sufficiently grave reason—is self-evident in the lethal nature of H.I.V. transmission.

Finally, our assistance must not be necessary for the illicit action to be carried out. Since exchange programs provide no means for injection that a drug user does not already have, N.E.P.'s meet the requirement that our cooperation be dispensable, not indispensable.

Steps Toward Recovery

This analysis suggests that permitting or even cooperating with N.E.P.'s would be allowed by traditional criteria, and that prudential judgment will be needed in each circumstance to determine the appropriate response of the local church. While toleration and cooperation can both be justified, I would propose that advocacy on behalf of N.E.P.'s is consistent with an ethics of mercy, with our traditional moral principles and with our pastoral mission to help the poor and marginalized. This approach recognizes that addiction is a disease whose natural history includes relapse, and it assists addicts in taking whatever small steps toward recovery are possible while protecting them and society from serious harm.

> *"By inhibiting users from possessing needles [existing drug paraphernalia laws] 'unwittingly contribute to the sharing of contaminated ones.'"*

I have asked many of my patients who became H.I.V.-infected through needle sharing how they regard exchange programs. While a few have been opposed—out of concern that they could send a mixed message—most wished that someone had cared enough for their welfare to make such an option available when they were in the throes of addiction, possibly preventing the life-threatening condition with which they now struggle.

N.E.P.'s Save Lives

I urge that we move beyond an understandable concern about sending mixed messages, to recognizing the central moral facts of the case. While neither condoning nor increasing drug use, N.E.P.'s save lives and bring addicts into treatment. A University of California study has calculated that up to 10,000 lives might have been saved thus far if we, as a nation, had supported needle exchange early on. It further estimated that "if current U.S. policies are not changed an additional 5,150–11,329 preventable H.I.V. infections could occur by the year 2000." Our mandate to provide special attention to the health and welfare needs of the most vulnerable must certainly include injection drug users and their children and sexual partners. Let us engage our considerable resources in examining and discussing this question, exploring how best to support recovery from addiction while protecting vulnerable lives from life-threatening disease.

The Effectiveness of Drug Treatment Has Not Been Proven

by Fred Reed

About the author: *Fred Reed is a syndicated columnist based in Washington, D.C.*

Are efforts at rehabilitating drug users worthwhile?

My guess is that they are not, but a guess is a poor basis for policy. We need to know. The trouble is in part that it is not easy to find reliable evaluations of rehab programs, and in part that so many people have agendas to promote.

Politicians know that nothing can be done to stop the flow of drugs into the United States. Smuggling is both too easy and too profitable for interdiction of supplies to work.

Imprisoning dealers and users doesn't work either. The jails already are bursting; and the costs, both political and financial, of building ever more cells do not permit much increase in incarceration, which quite likely wouldn't work anyway.

Politicians do not want to tell the public that nothing can be done about a problem that people regard as extremely serious. Nor do they want the heat that would come from stuffing an even larger proportion of the black population into jail.

Self-Contradictory Research

The easiest way out is to promote rehabilitation, which sounds compassionate and constructive and doesn't antagonize influential groups. Whether it works doesn't matter too much.

For some time, I have been hearing here and there about a 1994 study by RAND [Research and Development Corporation], which, according to some accounts, said that every dollar spent on rehab saves $7 in spending on such things as imprisonment and law enforcement.

From "Does Drug Rehab Work? Nobody Knows," by Fred Reed, *Metropolitan Times*, March 31, 1998.

RAND is usually good, so I got a copy of the study. It is, in fact, not a study of rehabilitation but an attempt to compare the dollar effectiveness of increasing spending on different approaches to the cocaine epidemic—e.g., of spending more on domestic interdiction, on eradication in the source countries, and so on.

The study is murky because it relies, having no choice, on soft data and assumptions that are plausible but not necessarily correct (a problem the authors note).

> *"The easiest way out is to promote rehabilitation. . . . Whether it works doesn't matter too much."*

Some of it seems self-contradictory: "An estimated 13 percent of heavy users treated do not return to heavy use after treatment. Although not all of these departures are permanent."

The study concludes, after warnings about the difficulty of estimating such things, that a dollar of rehab saves $7.46 in societal costs: crime, lost productivity, etc.

If so, fine. Let's rehabilitate like crazy.

Awash in Approximations

But the whole thing is so awash in approximations and extrapolations that it leaves the reader uneasy, and it doesn't square well with what I have seen in Washington, D.C.—residents of treatment programs coming out on the street to score, then going back in—or with regular assertions by cops that the city's rehab efforts are scams to make money for those who run them.

Whose data do you trust? How do you even get data?

For example, when a former addict leaves rehab, how does one even know where he is five years later, much less whether he is using? Presumably one doesn't simply call and ask. ("Oh, yeah, I'm smoking again. Come bust me for possession.")

It is a commonplace that Alcoholics Anonymous is effective in rehabilitating drunks. Narcotics Anonymous (NA) is said to do the same for addicts.

But if you look into these organizations, you find that they don't keep records of members (being, after all, anonymous), and don't even define "member."

Some people show up at NA for one night, others for a week or month or year. When they disappear, often no one knows whether they have gone back on drugs, moved, or quit and stayed clean. A few dedicated permanent members attribute their salvation, no doubt correctly, to NA—but the rate of success seems indeterminable.

The half-dozen publicly employed rehab counselors I have talked to have been almost evangelical in their enthusiasm, which is normal in the psychology industry—UFO-abduction therapists are equally convinced. The rehabilitators also tend to become angry when asked for evidence of effectiveness, which wouldn't be their reaction if they had much evidence.

A Need for Reliable Data

So . . . what are we getting for our rehab dollar? And how do we find out?

Somebody needs to put in the time to come up with reliable data. In particular, studies need control groups. How many addicts who want to be in rehab would quit by themselves? Nicotine addicts who quit usually do so on their own. How much more effective is rehab than nothing?

The answer might be surprising—to me, at any rate. Maybe it would turn out that rehab, or some particular form of rehab, actually works well, at least with certain kinds of addicts. But we need to know.

The DARE Program Has Not Been Effective

by Ryan H. Sager

About the author: *Ryan H. Sager is a journalist and research associate with the National Center for Public Policy Research, a nonprofit educational program in Washington, D.C.*

Visit a college party, and you're likely to see people smoking cigarettes, drinking alcohol—and, quite often, smoking pot and using various other drugs. This scene will horrify some, but it won't surprise anyone familiar with today's college-age youth. Even though the generation of students now in college is the first to have been exposed to anti-drug messages since birth, a large portion of them seem not to have been convinced. By age 18, about 55 percent of students have tried some illicit drug, and 26 percent of college-age kids report having used an illicit drug within the last month. These numbers are up significantly from the beginning of the 1990s. This drug use may or may not represent a serious problem—most of these people go on to lead decent, productive lives—but it does testify to the ineffectiveness of anti-drug education and advertising in this country.

At a time when educators and the federal government are as committed as ever to the public-private Drug Abuse Resistance Education (DARE) program, and to a new $1-billion five-year taxpayer-funded anti-drug advertising campaign, it is appropriate to evaluate the return we're getting on this investment. If you ask anti-drug activists, some will say these programs have had a demonstrable impact on young people's attitudes toward drugs as well as their use of drugs. Others, however, are concerned that these programs have not proven their worth and could be diverting resources from more effective ways of preventing drug use by young people. According to this view, the public-education front of the drug war has been little more than an expensive placebo.

No Long-Term Effect

DARE, which costs approximately $220 million a year (including $1.75 million in taxpayer funding), is by far the most popular anti-drug program in

American schools. About 75 percent of school districts use it. While parents and politicians tend to view DARE as sacred, most people are unaware that the program has long faced intense skepticism from experts. Although some studies have found positive effects (mostly attitude changes) over the short term, DARE has never been proven to have any lasting effect on the likeliness of children to use drugs later in life. Numerous studies, in fact, have found that the program has no long-term effect whatsoever. Sending police officers into classrooms to lecture children on the dangers of drugs—the gist of DARE's approach—may lower their opinions of drugs temporarily, but the lessons seem to fade quickly.

For years, DARE officials confronted with these negative studies have dismissed the studies as inadequate in scope. But a recent study by researchers at the University of Kentucky should put those objections to rest. The study examined a group of young people ten years after they completed the DARE curriculum and concluded that these students were just as likely to use drugs as a group of students who had been exposed to just a minimal drug-education curriculum in their health classes. Though DARE officials have complained that the study should have compared DARE students to students who had received no drug education at all, such a sample would be nearly impossible to find. Furthermore, the argument that DARE should be preserved even if it is no more effective than a shorter and less expensive program seems untenable.

"The public-education front of the drug war has been little more than an expensive placebo."

Charlie Parsons, executive director of DARE America, doesn't believe the University of Kentucky study. He claims the program's curriculum has changed significantly since the period when the tracked students had it, and he puts his own spin on the data: "The effects dissipate somewhat, and that's not a surprise. It shows there's a need for reinforcement, and we totally agree with that." He even offers a solution to any problem that may exist: Extend the DARE program. The students in the University of Kentucky study were exposed to DARE only in elementary school. Mr. Parsons points to a study from Ohio University that shows lower drug use among students who continue with DARE during middle school and high school.

The "No-Use" Approach

Despite Parsons's optimism, some researchers remain skeptical. Joel Brown, executive director of the Center for Educational Research and Development in Berkeley, questions the validity of the Ohio study on methodological grounds. He also notes that there is still no research showing that the program has any lasting effect.

More generally, Brown is skeptical of the "no-use" approach used by DARE and other programs. "The reality is that most kids will experiment with drugs," he says. He doesn't condone experimentation, but thinks a wiser approach would be "telling kids the truth about drugs, trusting young people's ability to make decisions if given information." Brown thinks that kids who are at risk, or who already have problems with drugs, are unable to get useful advice from a program like DARE and could end up in deep trouble. Furthermore, Brown fears that when young people

> *"DARE has never been proven to have any lasting effect on the likeliness of children to use drugs later in life."*

experiment with drugs (or observe others doing so) and find that the dire warnings they heard in DARE were overblown, they will feel that their elders have been lying to them for years. This, he says, could create "cognitive dissonance" that will lead them to reject not just the message but the messenger.

The new anti-drug advertising campaign has the same problem: It has little room for a balanced view of drugs and is, for the most part, a variation on the theme of "Just say no." "It's just trying to scare people into not using drugs," says Brown. "There's no evidence that it really has an impact."

Whether or not it has an impact, of course, is an important question, now that the federal government has embarked on a $1-billion ad campaign. But it is almost impossible to study the effects of such a nationwide campaign on kids, because there is no control group—no similar kids who have not seen the ads—to use for comparison.

Up to Parents

The Partnership for a Drug-Free America, the organization responsible for most of the anti-drug advertising on television, admits as much. Steve Dnistrian, a Partnership official, points to a correlation between anti-drug advertising and teenage drug use that he believes proves the effectiveness of the new ad campaign. "We're about two years into a very encouraging flattening, if not decline" in teenage drug use, he claims. In fact, according to the University of Michigan's annual Monitoring the Future study, from 1998 to 1999—the study's first opportunity to measure the effect of the new anti-drug ads—teen drug use actually increased (though to a lesser extent than in most years during the 1990s). More important, the flattening to which Dnistrian refers clearly predates the advertising campaign.

What is left after a careful examination of anti-drug education and advertising is a fairly bleak picture for the anti-drug forces. The most widely used drug-education program in America has never proven that it can prevent young people from using drugs, and evidence for the effectiveness of anti-drug advertising is circumstantial at best. Hundreds of millions of dollars go into these programs every year, yet no one can point to any concrete results.

The problem is an anti-drug establishment with no interest in reconsidering its message, or even how the message is delivered. Kids know that smoking one joint will not ruin their lives, so telling them that it will can only make them more cynical than they already are. What we need is a fundamental rethinking of how we talk to kids about drugs. The government is not likely to do this any-time soon—so in the short term, it will be up to parents, alone, to give their kids realistic advice on drugs.

Antidrug Media Campaigns Should Be Reevaluated

by S. Shyam Sundar

About the author: *S. Shyam Sundar is assistant professor and director of the Media Effects Research Laboratory, College of Communications, Pennsylvania State University.*

Although two decades of research has shown that anti-drug public service announcements (PSAs) are enormously successful in reaching the intended target audiences, and although PSAs are shown to promote anti-drug attitudes among our youth, we have not seen commensurate decreases in drug usage rates. In fact, we have seen increases in drug use among our youth over the years. These contradictory facts inspired us to pursue a novel line of research, namely the unintended effects of prosocial media messages. In particular, we wondered if anti-drug PSAs were somehow triggering cognitions that would influence behavior in an undesirable direction.

Knowledge-Attitude-Behavior

I interpret the contradictory findings from prior PSA research as yet another example of a breakdown in the traditional Knowledge-Attitude-Behavior (K-A-B) hierarchy of media effects. This hierarchy is premised on the belief that knowledge, attitudes, and behaviors are causally connected, and that, in order for us to change behaviors, we will have to first change knowledge and attitudes. In other words, the supposition is that *knowledge* that drugs are bad will lead to negative *attitudes* about drugs, which in turn will result in anti-drug *behaviors*. Despite lackluster empirical support, this theoretical formulation seems to be embraced whole-heartedly by advertisers, including apparently those that design PSAs—partly because there are no other seemingly plausible alternatives, but mostly because the K-A-B mechanism is so powerful in its intuitive appeal.

Excerpted from S. Shyam Sundar's testimony before the United States House of Representatives, House Committee on Government Reform, Subcommittee on Criminal Justice, Drug Policy, and Human Resources, October 14, 1999.

Viewed from the K-A-B perspective, the contradiction in the effects of anti-drug PSAs lies in the link between attitudes and behaviors. Since drug-related attitudes have already been extensively studied by others and shown expected results, we set out to explore behavioral indicators in our research. Since it is next to impossible to measure behaviors as a direct consequence of exposure to media messages, we focused on measures of what we call conation, i.e., behavioral intention.

Priming the Viewers

In our theoretical explorations, we found the variable of "conative curiosity" to be particularly intriguing. We hypothesized that anti-drug PSAs would "prime" viewers to think about drugs, bringing to mind drug-related thoughts stored previously, and leading them to cognitively exaggerate the prevalence of drug use in society. Such a perception of exaggerated norm would then lead to a perceived gap in information (i.e., others seem to know more about drugs than me), followed by a drive to narrow this gap by gaining experiential knowledge, thereby resulting in an expression of curiosity about experimenting with drugs.

We proceeded to test this hypothesis through a simple experiment involving 65 high-school seniors as participants in one of two conditions. Participants in the control condition saw an unaltered version of a prime-time television program complete with commercial breaks, while those in the experimental condition saw the

> *"Although PSAs (public service announcements) are shown to promote anti-drug attitudes among our youth, we have not seen commensurate decreases in drug usage rates."*

same program, but with four anti-drug PSAs edited into the commercial breaks. Following the program, participants in both conditions filled out an identical questionnaire containing, among other things, five items that elicited their level of curiosity toward illicit drugs. These five questionnaire items were in the form of statements, and participants were asked to indicate their level of agreement with each one of them:

1. There are no benefits to using marijuana.
2. Marijuana use is associated with a weak will.
3. It would be interesting to know what using marijuana feels like.
4. It might be interesting to try marijuana.
5. Using marijuana might be fun.

Higher the participants' scores on items 3 through 5 and lower their scores on items 1 and 2, greater is their level of curiosity.

Increasing Curiosity

We found that participants in the experimental condition (i.e., the high-school seniors who saw the program with the four anti-drug PSAs) expressed significantly greater curiosity than their counterparts in the control condition (i.e., those who did not see the PSAs). We also found that they tended to exaggerate the norm of drug use. Compared to those in the control condition, participants in the treatment condition gave significantly higher estimates when asked for the percentage of high school-students who have used marijuana in the past year and the past month. We, however, did not find a significant relationship between these perceptions of norms and level of curiosity.

> *"We hypothesized that anti-drug PSAs would 'prime' viewers to think about drugs."*

Therefore, it appears that anti-drug PSAs independently increase both curiosity about drugs and perceived prevalence of drug use. But, this is only a modest first attempt at showing a relationship, and the results should be viewed with skepticism until more evidence is generated.

A few caveats must be kept in mind while interpreting these findings. The study we conducted is an experiment with a small sample in a controlled setting. While experiments of this kind have the advantage of demonstrating causation between variables, it would be premature to generalize their findings to the real world without extensive further study. My co-author and student, Carson Wagner, replicated the experiment in the Spring of 1999 in a different state with a slightly older sample of 28 participants, and using a different set of PSAs. Unpublished data from this replication indicate again that those who were exposed to PSAs expressed greater curiosity toward drugs than their counterparts not shown the PSAs. Moreover, they showed a higher acceptance of experimentation with drugs. Similarly other researchers, using [a] different sample of participants as well as PSAs, would have to replicate the study before we can declare this a robust effect of anti-drug PSAs. In addition, future research should examine the duration of the curiosity-arousing effect. Our experiments only measured immediate effects, not long-term effects. We have also not established a connection between curiosity and actual behavior.

The "Forbidden Fruit" Effect

Clearly, our research raises more questions than it answers. This exploratory piece of research has brought to the fore the potential of PSAs to arouse curiosity, but our data are unable to specify the exact theoretical mechanism by which exposure to PSAs affects one's level of conative curiosity. In our paper, we discuss a number of possibilities, such as the absence of resolution and violation of expectations in PSAs leading to some of the demonstrated effects, but these are merely speculative at this point. Others have suggested that this could be an example of the "forbidden fruit" effect, i.e., the tendency among adolescents to be drawn toward that which is forbidden or taboo. Future research can explore these possibilities.

By presenting our findings, we are certainly *not* claiming that curiosity is the only outcome of anti-drug PSAs. This just happens to be the variable we examined. There could be many other variables that indicate positive outcomes, as other researchers have shown, which may have far greater beneficial effects on our youth than the potential negative consequences of arousing curiosity.

We are also *not* recommending that national anti-drug media campaigns be abandoned, as has been incorrectly implied in certain media reports of our study. If anything, we are very interested in ensuring that such campaigns have the intended pro-social effects by minimizing their potential, if any, to have unintended negative consequences.

Our research has implications for at least two areas of current anti-drug media campaigns. They are: Message Design and Evaluation.

Since our findings raise the possibility that a mere mention of drugs can serve to prime audience members to think about drugs when it wasn't there before (potentially leading to unintended message effects), an immediate suggestion would be to design PSAs that provide our youngsters with examples of alternative activities that are healthy and can take the place of drugs in their lives. However, as my co-author Carson Wagner mentioned during the presentation of this study at the International Communication Association, the fact that these are *alternative* activities cannot be explicitly mentioned because this requires identifying that to which the activities are alternative, namely drugs. This is where the message designers have to get creative.

Fear Appeals

Another implication for message design suggested by our study is a move away from the Fried-Egg paradigm of social marketing. The genre of ads that promote the brain-on-drugs message, including the recent Frying Pan advertisement, is enormously effective in that it powerfully attracts audience attention. In fact, advertising classes in communication schools use these types of ads as good examples for promoting what they call TOMA (Top-Of-Mind Awareness). While TOMA is desirable for commercial products because it promotes brand identification in grocery store aisles, it may be inappropriate for advocating preventive health behaviors because it might needlessly make salient unhealthy behaviors. Social psychologists call these ads Fear Appeals. While fear appeals have been shown to have good recall rates among viewers, our research suggests that they might trigger curiosity. Most of the ads used in our experiments were fear-appeal ads, and perhaps the curiosity effect we discovered is due to this kind of appeal. There are other health communication models available for message design, such as health belief model and social learning theory, which may result in different

> *"It appears that anti-drug PSAs independently increase both curiosity about drugs and perceived prevalence of drug use."*

types of message elaboration in the minds of viewers, leading perhaps to desirable behaviors. Future research should be directed toward discovering those appeals that optimally produce desired positive outcomes while minimizing undesirable negative consequences.

Implications for Evaluation

In addition to motivating a closer look at message design, our research has implications for evaluation research. In particular, it demonstrates the need for controlled laboratory and field experimentation in order to isolate outcome variables such as curiosity. Our research demonstrates a departure from prior PSA research—not just because it measured unintended negative effects of well-intentioned media messages (these effects are usually measured as a function of clearly anti-social entertainment genres such as sex and violence on television), but because it showed differences in effects as a function of the very existence of PSAs. This is in contrast to traditional experimental research in the area that assesses the relative effects of two or more PSAs (i.e., participants in different experimental groups are shown different PSAs) without a pure control condition that has no exposure to PSAs.

The larger implication for evaluation is that our study calls for more research on effects of PSAs in particular, not just PSA campaigns in general. The latter is achieved through large-sample surveys and can produce useful correlational data, but we can never be sure if survey respondents were ever really exposed to the PSAs and if so, which particular ones, and whether and how they were directly affected by it. Moreover, given the sensitive nature of the subject matter, survey respondents could be prone to give socially desirable answers to researchers. Small-sample experiments, on the other hand, can ensure exposure and measure effects in a controlled fashion, but their generalizability is suspect. Of course, both methods have their pros and cons. Ideally, a combination of experiments and surveys should be used to evaluate the overall effectiveness of anti-drug media campaigns.

Needle-Exchange Programs Do Not Reduce the Harms of Intravenous Drug Use

by James L. Curtis

About the author: *James L. Curtis is director of psychiatry at Harlem Hospital in New York and a psychiatry professor at Columbia University.*

Donna Shalala, the Secretary of Health and Human Services, wanted it both ways in April 1998. She announced that Federal money would not be used for programs that distribute clean needles to addicts. But she offered only a half-hearted defense of that decision, even stating that while the Clinton Administration would not finance such programs, it supported them in theory.

Ms. Shalala should have defended the Administration's decision vigorously. Instead, she chose to placate AIDS activists, who insist that giving free needles to addicts is a cheap and easy way to prevent H.I.V. infection.

Simplistic Nonsense

This is simplistic nonsense that stands common sense on its head. For the past 10 years, as a black psychiatrist specializing in addiction, I have warned about the dangers of needle-exchange policies, which hurt not only individual addicts but also poor and minority communities.

There is no evidence that such programs work. Take a look at the way many of them are conducted in the United States. An addict is enrolled anonymously, without being given an H.I.V. test to determine whether he or she is already infected. The addict is given a coded identification card exempting him or her from arrest for carrying drug paraphernalia. There is no strict accounting of how many needles are given out or returned.

How can such an effort prove it is preventing the spread of H.I.V. if the participants are anonymous and if they aren't tested for the virus before and after entering the program?

Studies in Montreal and Vancouver did systematically test participants in needle-exchange programs. And the studies found that those addicts who took part in such exchanges were two to three times more likely to become infected with H.I.V. than those who did not participate. They also found that almost half the addicts frequently shared needles with others anyway.

This was unwelcome news to the AIDS establishment. For almost two years, the Montreal study was not reported in scientific journals. After the study finally appeared in a medical journal, two of the researchers, Julie Bruneau and Martin T. Schechter, said that their results had been misinterpreted. The results, they said, needed to be seen in the context of H.I.V. rates in other inner-city neighborhoods. They even suggested that maybe the number of needles given out in Vancouver should be raised to 10 million from 2 million.

The Lure of Free Needles

Needle-exchange programs are reckless experiments. Clearly there is more than a minimal risk of contracting the virus. And addicts already infected with H.I.V., or infected while in the program, are not given antiretroviral medications, which we know combats the virus in its earliest stages.

Needle exchanges also affect poor communities adversely. For instance, the Lower East Side Harm Reduction Center is one of New York City's largest needle-exchange programs. According to tenant groups I have talked to, the center, since it began in 1992, has become a magnet not only for addicts but for dealers as well. Used needles, syringes and crack vials litter the sidewalk. Tenants who live next door to the center complain that the police don't arrest addicts who hang out near it, even though they are openly buying drugs and injecting them.

The indisputable fact is that needle exchanges merely help addicts continue to use drugs. It's not unlike giving an alcoholic a clean Scotch tumbler to prevent meningitis. Drug addicts suffer from a serious disease requiring comprehensive treatment, sometimes under compulsion. Ultimately, that's the best way to reduce H.I.V. infection among this group. What addicts don't need is the lure of free needles.

Chapter 4

Should Drug Policies Be Liberalized?

Chapter Preface

In 1985, the U.S. government spent $2.5 billion waging the war on drugs. Five years later, that figure had nearly quadrupled to $9.7 billion. In 2000, federal spending on antidrug efforts reached $17 billion, the highest in the drug war's thirty-year history.

Detractors of America's current drug policy claim that the costly drug war is failing to reduce drug abuse and wasting money that could be effectively used to fight other social problems. Others, compelled by the fact that the illegal drug trade is projected to be a $400-billion-a-year industry, contend that legalizing and taxing the sale of drugs could offer a more cost-effective way to deal with the drug problem. According to biblical professor Walter Wink, "Taxes on drugs would pay for enforcement, education, rehabilitation, and research (a net benefit is estimated of at least $10 billion from reduced expenditures on enforcement and new tax revenues)."

However, supporters of the drug war assert that legalizing drugs would result in economic disaster. If drugs were legalized, they claim that drug use would increase and raise the already enormous financial cost of dealing with problems associated with drug use. Barry R. McCaffrey, former director of the Office of National Drug Control Policy, states, "Drug legalization would cost billions of dollars and risk additional innocent lives." In addition, he contends that the "increasing rates of drug use burden our economy as a whole. They place businesses, small businesses in particular, at risk. In the end, it is the American consumer who ultimately pays these costs."

In the following viewpoints, the authors debate whether the price of the drug war is greater or less than the consequences of drug abuse itself.

Drug Use Should Be Legalized

by Gary E. Johnson

About the author: *Gary E. Johnson is governor of New Mexico.*

I am a "cost-benefit" analysis person. What's the cost and what's the benefit? A couple of things scream out as failing cost-benefit criteria. One is education. The other is the war on drugs. We are presently spending $50 billion a year to combat drugs. I'm talking about police, courts, and jails. For the amount of money that we're putting into it, I want to suggest, the war on drugs is an absolute failure. My "outrageous" hypothesis is that under a legalized scenario, we could actually hold drug use level or see it decline.

Sometimes people say to me, "Governor, I am absolutely opposed to your stand on drugs." I respond by asking them, "You're for drugs, you want to see kids use drugs?" Let me make something clear. I'm not pro-drug. I'm against drugs. Don't do drugs. Drugs are a real handicap. Don't do alcohol or tobacco, either. They are real handicaps.

There's another issue beyond cost-benefit criteria. Should you go to jail for using drugs? And I'm not talking about doing drugs and committing a crime or driving a car. Should you go to jail for simply doing drugs? I say no, you shouldn't. People ask me, "What do you tell kids?" Well, you tell the truth: that by legalizing drugs, we can control them, regulate and tax them. If we legalize drugs, we might have a healthier society. And you explain how that might take place. But you emphasize that drugs are a bad choice. Don't do drugs. But if you do, we're not going to throw you in jail for it.

New Laws and Problems

If drugs are legalized, there will be a whole new set of laws. Let me mention a few of them. Let's say you can't do drugs if you're under 21. You can't sell drugs to kids. I say employers should be able to discriminate against drug users. Employers should be able to conduct drug tests, and they should not have to comply with the Americans with Disabilities Act. Do drugs and commit a crime? Make it like a gun. Enhance the penalty for the crime in the same way we do today with guns. Do drugs and drive? There should be a law similar to one we have now for driving under the influence of alcohol.

I propose that we redirect the $50 billion that we're presently spending (state and federal) on the old laws to enforce a new set of laws. Society would be transformed if law enforcement could focus on crimes other than drug use. Police could crack down on speeding violations, burglaries, and other offenses that law enforcement now lacks the opportunity to enforce.

Half the Negative Consequences

If drugs are legalized, there will be a new set of problems, but they will have only about half the negative consequence of those we have today. A legalization model will be a dynamic process that will be fine-tuned as we go along.

Does anybody want to press a button that would retroactively punish the 80 million Americans who have done illegal drugs over the years? I might point out that I'm one of those individuals. In running for my first term in office, I offered the fact that I had smoked marijuana. And the media were very quick to say, "Oh, so you experimented with marijuana?" "No," I said, "I smoked marijuana!" This is something I did, along with a lot of other people. I look back on it now, and I view drugs as a handicap. I stopped because it was a handicap. The same with drinking and tobacco. But did my friends and I belong in jail? I don't think that we should continue to lock up Americans because of bad choices.

And what about the bad choices regarding alcohol and tobacco? I've heard people say, "Governor, you're not comparing alcohol to drugs? You're not comparing tobacco to drugs?" I say, "Hell no! Alcohol killed 150,000 people last year. And I'm not talking about drinking and driving. I'm just talking about the health effects. The health effects of tobacco killed 450,000 people last year." I don't mean to be flippant, but I don't know of anybody ever dying from a marijuana overdose.

Less Lethal than Alcohol

I understand that 2,000 to 3,000 people died in 1998 from abusing cocaine and heroine. If drugs were legalized, those deaths would go away, theoretically speaking, because they would no longer be counted as accidental. Instead, they'd be suicides, because in a legalized scenario drugs are controlled, taxed, and properly understood. I want to be so bold as to say that marijuana is never going to have the devastating effects on society that alcohol has had.

My own informal poll among doctors reveals that 75–80 percent of the patients they examine have health-related problems due to alcohol and tobacco. My brother is a cardiothoracic surgeon who performs heart transplants. He says that 80 percent of the problems he sees are alcohol and tobacco related. He sees about six people a year who have infected heart valves because of intravenous drug use, but the infection isn't from the drugs themselves. It's the dirty needles that cause the health problems.

Marijuana is said to be a gateway drug. We all know that, right? You're 85 times more likely to do cocaine if you do marijuana. I don't mean to be flippant, but 100 percent of all substance abuse starts with milk. You've heard it, but that bears repeating. My new mantra here is "Just Say Know." Just know that there are two sides to all these arguments. I think the facts boil down to drugs being a bad choice. But should someone go to jail for just doing drugs? That is the reality of what is happening today. I believe the time has come for that to end.

A Muddy Term

I've been talking about legalization and not decriminalization. Legalization means we educate, regulate, tax, and control the estimated $400 billion a year drug industry. That's larger than the automobile industry. Decriminalization is a muddy term. It turns its back to half the problems involved in getting the entire drug economy above the line. So that's why I talk about legalization, meaning control, the ability to tax, regulate, and educate.

> *"My 'outrageous' hypothesis is that under a legalized scenario, we could actually hold drug use level or see it decline."*

We need to make drugs controlled substances just like alcohol. Perhaps we ought to let the government regulate them; let the government grow or manufacture, distribute and market them. If that doesn't lead to decreased drug use, I don't know what would!

Kids today will tell you that legal prescription drugs are harder to come by than illegal drugs. Well, of course. To get legal drugs, you must walk into a pharmacy and show identification. It's the difference between a controlled substance and an illegal substance. A teenager today will tell you that a bottle of beer is harder to come by than a joint. That's where we've come to today. It's where we've come to with regard to controlling alcohol, but it shows how out of control drugs have become.

Not Driving You Crazy

Drug Czar Barry McCaffrey has made me his poster child for drug legalization. He claims that drug use has been cut in half and that we are winning the drug war. Well, let's assume that we have cut it in half. I don't buy that for a minute, but let's assume that it's true. Consider these facts: In the late 1970s the federal government spent a billion dollars annually on the drug war. Today, the feds are spending $19 billion a year on it. In the late 1970s, we were arresting a few hundred thousand people. Today, we're arresting 1.6 million. Does that mean if drug use declines by half from today's levels, we'll spend $38 billion federally and arrest 3.2 million people annually? I mean, to follow that logic, when we're left with a few hundred users nationwide, the entire gross national product will be devoted to drug-law enforcement!

Most people don't understand, as we New Mexicans do, that the mules are carrying the drugs in. I'm talking about Mexican citizens who are paid a couple hundred dollars to bring drugs across the border, and they don't even know who has given them the money. They just know that it's a king's ransom and that there are more than enough Mexican citizens willing to do it. The federal government is catching many of the mules and some of the kingpins. Let's not deny that. But those who are caught, those links out of the chain, don't make any difference in the overall war on drugs.

> *"If we legalize drugs, we might have a healthier society."*

Stop Locking Up the Country

I want to tell you a little bit about the response to what I've been saying. Politically, this is a zero. For anybody holding office, for anybody who aspires to hold office, has held office, or has a job associated with politics, this is verboten. I am in the ground, and the dirt is being thrown on top of my coffin. But among the public, the response is overwhelming. In New Mexico, I am being approached rapid-fire by people saying "right on" to my statements regarding the war on drugs. To give an example, two elderly ladies came up to my table during dinner the other night. They said, "We're teachers, and we think your school voucher idea sucks. But your position on the war on drugs is right on!"

What I have discovered, and it's been said before, is that the war on drugs is thousands of miles long, but it's only about a quarter-inch deep. I'm trying to communicate what I believe in this issue. Drugs are bad, but we need to stop arresting and locking up the entire country.

Marijuana Should Be Legalized

by R. Keith Stroup

About the author: *R. Keith Stroup is executive director of the National Organization for the Reform of Marijuana Laws (NORML), an organization that supports the decriminalization of marijuana use.*

Current marijuana policy is a dismal and costly failure. It wastes untold billions of dollars in law enforcement resources, and needlessly wrecks the lives and careers of millions of our citizens. Yet marijuana remains the recreational drug of choice for millions of Americans.

Congress needs to move beyond the "reefer madness" phase of our marijuana policy, where elected officials attempt to frighten Americans into supporting the status quo by exaggerating marijuana's potential dangers. This is an issue about which most members of Congress are simply out of touch with their constituents, who know the difference between marijuana and more dangerous drugs, and who oppose spending $25,000 a year to jail an otherwise law-abiding marijuana smoker.

In fact, if marijuana smoking were dangerous, we would certainly know it; a significant segment of our population currently smoke marijuana recreationally, and there would be epidemiological evidence of harm among real people. No such evidence exists, despite millions of people who have smoked marijuana for years. So while we do need to fund more research on marijuana, especially research regarding medical uses—which, by the way, has been delayed by the federal government for years—we certainly know marijuana is relatively safe when used responsibly by adults.

It's time for Congress to let go of reefer madness, to end the crusade against marijuana and marijuana smokers, and to begin to deal with marijuana policy in a rational manner. The debate over marijuana policy in this Congress needs to be expanded beyond the current parameters to include consideration of (1) decriminalizing the marijuana smoker and (2) legalizing and regulating the sale of marijuana to eliminate the black market.

Excerpted from R. Keith Stroup's testimony before the United States House of Representatives, House Committee on Government Reform, Subcommittee on Criminal Justice, Drug Policy, and Human Resources, July 13, 1999.

Not a Deviant Activity

It is time to put to rest the myth that smoking marijuana is a fringe or deviant activity engaged in only by those on the margins of American society. In reality, marijuana smoking is extremely common and marijuana is the recreational drug of choice for millions of mainstream, middle class Americans. Government's surveys indicate more than 70 million Americans have smoked marijuana at some point in their lives, and that 18–20 million have smoked during the last year. Marijuana is the third most popular recreational drug of choice for Americans, exceeded only by alcohol and tobacco in popularity.

A national survey of voters conducted by the American Civil Liberties Union (ACLU) found that 32%—one third of the voting adults in the country—acknowledged having smoked marijuana at some point in their lives. Many successful business and professional leaders, including many state and federal elected officials from both political parties, admit they used marijuana. It is time to reflect that reality in our state and federal legislation, and stop acting as if marijuana smokers are part of the crime problem. They are not, and it is absurd to continue spending limited law enforcement resources arresting them.

Like most Americans, the vast majority of these millions of marijuana smokers are otherwise law-abiding citizens who work hard, raise families and contribute to their communities; they are indistinguishable from their non-smoking peers, except for their use of marijuana. They are not part of the crime problem and should not be treated like criminals. Arresting and jailing responsible marijuana smokers is a misapplication of the criminal sanction which undermines respect for the law in general.

> *"Current marijuana policy is a dismal and costly failure."*

Congress needs to acknowledge this constituency exists, and stop legislating as if marijuana smokers were dangerous people who need to be locked up. Marijuana smokers are simply average Americans.

Marijuana Arrests Have Skyrocketed

Current enforcement policies seem focused on arresting marijuana smokers. The FBI reports that police arrested 695,000 Americans, the highest number ever recorded, on marijuana charges in 1997 (the latest year for which data are available), and more than 3.7 million Americans this decade; *83% of these arrests were for simple possession, not sale.* Presently one American is arrested on marijuana charges every 45 seconds. Approximately 44% of all drug arrests in this country are marijuana arrests. Despite criticism from some in Congress that President Clinton is "soft" on drugs, annual data from the Federal Bureau of Investigation's (FBI) Uniform Crime Report demonstrate that Clinton administration officials are waging a more intensive war on marijuana smokers than any other presidency in history. Marijuana arrests have more than doubled since President Clinton took office. This reality appears to conflict with recent statements by White House Drug Czar Barry McCaffrey that America "can not arrest our way out of the drug problem."

Unfortunately, this renewed focus on marijuana smokers represents a shift away from enforcement against more dangerous drugs such as cocaine and heroin. Specifically, marijuana arrests have more than doubled since 1990 while the percentage of arrests for the sale of cocaine and heroin have fallen 51%. Drug arrests have increased 31% in the last decade, and the increase in marijuana arrests accounts for most of that increase.

Marijuana Penalties Cause Enormous Harm

Marijuana penalties vary nationwide, but most levy a heavy financial and social impact for the hundreds of thousands of Americans who are arrested each year. In 42 states, possession of any amount of marijuana is punishable by incarceration and/or a significant fine. Many states also have laws automatically suspending the drivers' license of an individual if they are convicted of any marijuana offense, even if the offense was not driving related.

Penalties for marijuana cultivation and/or sale also vary from state to state. Ten states have maximum sentences of five years or less and eleven states have a maximum penalty of thirty years or more. Some states punish those who cultivate marijuana solely for personal use as severely as large scale traffickers. For instance, medical marijuana user William Foster of Oklahoma was sentenced to 93 years in jail in January 1997 for growing 10 medium-sized marijuana plants and 56 clones (cuttings from another plant planted in soil) in a 25-square-foot underground shelter. Foster maintains that he grew marijuana to alleviate the pain of rheumatoid arthritis. Unfortunately, Foster's plight is not an isolated event; marijuana laws in six states permit marijuana importers and traffickers to be sentenced to life in jail.

Federal laws prohibiting marijuana are also severe. Under federal law, possessing one marijuana cigarette or less is punishable by a fine of up to $10,000 and one year in prison, the

> *"We certainly know marijuana is relatively safe when used responsibly by adults."*

same penalty as for possessing small amounts of heroin and cocaine. In one extreme case, attorney Edward Czuprynski of Michigan served 14 months in federal prison for possession of 1.6 grams of marijuana before a panel of federal appellate judges reviewed his case and demanded his immediate release. Cultivation of 100 marijuana plants or more carries a mandatory prison term of five years. Large scale marijuana cultivators and traffickers may be sentenced to death.

Not an Appropriate Response

Federal laws also deny entitlements to marijuana smokers. Under legislation signed into law in 1996 states may deny cash aid (e.g., welfare, etc.) and food stamps to anyone convicted of felony drug charges. For marijuana smokers, this includes most convictions for cultivation and sale, even for small amounts and nonprofit transfers. More recently, Congress passed amendments in 1998 to the Higher Education Act which deny federal financial aid to any student with any drug conviction, even for a single marijuana cigarette. No other class of offense, including violent offenses, predatory offenses or alcohol-related offenses, carries automatic denial of federal financial aid eligibility. While substance abuse among our young people is a cause for concern, closing the doors of our colleges and universities, making it more difficult for at-risk young people to succeed, is not an appropriate response to a college student with a minor marijuana conviction.

> *"It's time for Congress to let go of reefer madness, to end the crusade against marijuana and marijuana smokers."*

Even those who avoid incarceration are subject to an array of punishments that may include submitting to random drug tests, probation, paying for mandatory drug counseling, loss of an occupational license, expensive legal fees, lost wages due to absence from work, loss of child custody, loss of federal benefits, and removal from public housing. In some states, police will notify the employer of people who are arrested, which frequently results in the loss of employment.

In addition, under both state and federal law, mere investigation for a marijuana offense can result in the forfeiture of property, including cash, cars, boats, land, business equipment, and houses. The owner does not have to be found guilty or even formally charged with any crime for the seizure to occur; 80% of those whose property is seized are never charged with a crime. Law enforcement can target suspected marijuana offenders for the purpose of seizing their property, sometimes with tragic results. For example, millionaire rancher Donald Scott was shot and killed by law enforcement officials in 1992 at his Malibu estate in a botched raid. Law enforcement failed to find any marijuana plants growing on his property and later conceded that their primary motivation for investigating Scott was to eventually seize his land.

State and federal marijuana laws also have a disparate racial impact on ethnic minorities. While blacks and Hispanics make up only 20 percent of the marijuana smokers in the U.S., they comprised 58 percent of the marijuana offenders sentenced under federal law in 1995. State arrest and incarceration rates paint a similar portrait. For example, in Illinois, 57 percent of those sent to prison for marijuana in 1995 were black or Hispanic. In California, 49 percent of those arrested for marijuana offenses in 1994 were black or Hispanic. And in New York state, 71 percent of those arrested for misdemeanor marijuana charges in 1995 were nonwhite.

Arresting and jailing otherwise law-abiding citizens who smoke marijuana is a wasteful and incredibly destructive policy. It wastes valuable law enforcement resources that should be focused on violent and serious crime; it invites government into areas of our private lives that are inappropriate; and it frequently destroys the lives, careers and families of genuinely good citizens. It is time to end marijuana prohibition.

A Commonsense Option

In 1972, a blue-ribbon panel of experts appointed by President Richard Nixon and led by former Pennsylvania Governor Raymond Shafer concluded that marijuana prohibition posed significantly greater harm to the user than the use of marijuana itself. The National Commission on Marijuana and Drug Abuse recommended that state and federal laws be changed to remove criminal penalties for possession of marijuana for personal use and for the casual distribution of small amounts of marijuana. The report served as the basis for decriminalization bills adopted legislatively in 11 states during the 1970s.

A number of other prestigious governmental commissions have examined this issue over the last 25 years, and virtually all have reached the same conclusion: the purported dangers of marijuana smoking have been greatly overblown and the private use of marijuana by adults should not be a criminal matter. What former President Jimmy Carter said in a message to Congress in 1977, citing a key finding of the Marijuana Commission, is equally true today: "Penalties against drug use should not be more damaging to an individual than the use of the drug itself. Nowhere is this more clear than in the laws against possession of marijuana in private for personal use."

Favorable Experience with Decriminalization

Led by Oregon in 1973, 11 states adopted policies during the 1970s that removed criminal penalties for minor marijuana possession offenses and substituted a small civil fine enforced with a citation instead of an arrest. Today, approximately 30% of the population of this country live under some type of marijuana decriminalization law, and their experience has been favorable. The only U.S. federal study ever to compare marijuana use patterns among decriminalized states and those that have not found, "Decriminalization has had virtually no effect on either marijuana use or on related attitudes about marijuana use among young people." Dozens of privately commissioned follow up studies from the U.S. and abroad confirm this fact.

> *"Arresting and jailing responsible marijuana smokers is a misapplication of the criminal sanction."*

Decriminalization laws are popular with the voters, as evidenced by a 1998 state-wide vote in Oregon in which Oregonians voted 2 to 1 to reject a proposal, earlier adopted by their legislature, that would have reimposed criminal penalties for marijuana smokers. Oregonians clearly wanted to retain the decriminalization law that had worked well for nearly 30 years.

Since the Shafer Commission reported their findings to Congress in 1972 advocating marijuana decriminalization, over ten million Americans have been arrested on marijuana charges. Marijuana prohibition is a failed public policy that is out of touch with today's social reality and inflicts devastating harm on millions of citizens.

No Interest of the Government

It is time we adopted a marijuana policy that recognizes a distinction between use and abuse, and reflects the importance most Americans place on the right of the individual to be free from the overreaching power of government. Most would agree that the government has no business knowing what books we read, the subject of our telephone conversations, or how we conduct ourselves in the bedroom. Similarly, whether one smokes marijuana or drinks alcohol to relax is simply not an appropriate area of concern for the government.

By stubbornly defining all marijuana smoking as criminal, including that which involves adults smoking in the privacy of their home, government is wasting police and prosecutorial resources, clogging courts, filling costly and scarce jail and prison space, and needlessly wrecking the lives and careers of genuinely good citizens.

It is time that Congress acknowledge what millions of Americans know to be true: there is nothing wrong with the responsible use of marijuana by adults and it should be of no interest or concern to the government.

In the final analysis, this debate is only incidentally about marijuana; it is really about personal freedom.

Drug Use Should Be an Individual Choice

by Thomas Szasz

About the author: *Thomas Szasz is professor emeritus of psychiatry at Syracuse University in New York.*

Drug prohibitionists were alarmed in November 1996, when voters in Arizona and California endorsed the initiatives permitting the use of marijuana for "medical purposes." Opponents of drug prohibition ought to be even more alarmed: The advocates of medical marijuana have embraced a tactic that retards the repeal of drug prohibition and reinforces the moral legitimacy of prevailing drug policies. Instead of steadfastly maintaining that the War on Drugs is an intrinsically evil enterprise, the reformers propose replacing legal sanctions with medical tutelage, a principle destined to further expand the medical control of everyday behavior.

Not surprisingly, the drug prohibition establishment reacted to the passage of the marijuana initiatives as the Vatican might react to an outbreak of heretical schism. Senator Orrin G. Hatch, chairman of the Senate Judiciary Committee, declared: "We can't let this go without a response." Arizona Senator Jon Kyl told the Judiciary Committee: "I am extraordinarily embarrassed," adding that he believed most Arizona voters who supported the initiative "were deceived." Naturally. Only a person who had fallen into error could approve of sin. Too many critics of the War on Drugs continue to refuse to recognize that their adversaries are priests waging a holy war on Satanic chemicals, not statesmen who respect the people and whose sole aim is to give them access to the best possible information concerning the benefits and risks of biologically active substances.

Responsibility for Personal Conduct

From Colonial times until 1914, Americans were the authors of their own drug policy: they decided what substances to avoid or use, controlled the drug-using behavior of their children, and assumed responsibility for their personal conduct. Since 1914, the control of, and responsibility for, drug use—by adults as well as children—has been gradually transferred from citizens to agents of the state, principally physicians.

Supporters of the marijuana initiatives portray their policies as acts of compassion "to help the chronically or terminally ill." James E. Copple, president of Community Anti-Drug Coalitions of America, counters: "They are using the AIDS victims and terminally ill as props to promote the use of marijuana." He is right. Former Surgeon General Jocelyn Elders declares: "I think that we can really legalize marijuana." If by "legalizing" she means repealing marijuana prohibition, then she does not know what she is talking about. We have sunk so low in the War on Drugs that, at present, legalizing marijuana in the United States is about as practical as is legalizing Scotch in Saudi Arabia. A 1995 Gallup Poll found that 85 percent of the respondents opposed legalizing illicit drugs.

> *"From Colonial times until 1914, Americans were the authors of their own drug policy."*

Supporters of the marijuana initiatives are posturing as advocates of medical "responsibility" toward "sick patients." Physicians complain of being deprived of their right to free speech. It won't work. The government can out-responsible the doctors any day. Physicians have "prescription privileges," a euphemism for what is, in effect, the power to issue patients *ad hoc* licenses to buy certain drugs. This makes doctors major players in the state apparatus denying people their right to drugs, thereby denying them the option of responsible drug use and abdicating their own responsibilities to the government: "We will not turn a blind eye toward our responsibility," declared Attorney General Janet Reno at a news conference on December 30, 1996, where the Administration announced "that doctors in California and Arizona who ordered for their patients any drugs like marijuana . . . could lose their prescription privileges and even face criminal charges." I don't blame the doctors for wanting to forget the Satanic pact they have forged with the state, but they should not expect the government not to remind them of it.

"Rational Policy"

The American people as well as their elected representatives support the War on Drugs. The mainstream media addresses the subject in a language that precludes rational debate: crimes related to drug prohibition are systematically described as "drug-related." Perhaps most important, Americans in ever-increasing numbers seem to be deeply, almost religiously, committed to a medicalized view of life. Thus, Dennis Peron, the originator of the California marijuana proposition, believes that since relieving stress is beneficial to health, "any adult who uses marijuana does so for medical reasons." Similarly, Ethan Nadelmann, director of the Lindesmith Center (the George Soros think tank for drug policy), states: "The next step is toward arguing for a more rational drug policy," such as distributing hypodermic needles and increasing access to methadone for heroin addicts. These self-declared opponents of the War on Drugs are blind to the fatal compromise entailed in their use of the phrase "rational policy."

If we believe we have a right to a free press, we do not seek a rational book policy or reading policy; on the contrary, we would call such a policy "censorship" and a denial of our First Amendment rights.

If we believe we have a right to freedom of religion, we do not seek a rational belief policy or religion policy; on the contrary, we would call such a policy "religious persecution" and a denial of the constitutionally mandated separation of church and state.

Misranking the Government

So long as we do not believe in freedom of, and responsibility for, drug use, we cannot mount an effective opposition to medical-statist drug controls. In a free society, the duty of the government is to protect individuals from others who might harm them; it is not the government's business to protect individuals from harming themselves. Misranking these governmental functions precludes the possibility of repealing our drug laws. Presciently, C.S. Lewis warned against yielding to the temptations of medical tutelage: "Of all the tyrannies a tyranny sincerely exercised for the good of its victims may be the most oppressive. . . .

> *"Physicians have 'prescription privileges,' . . . the power to issue patients* **ad hoc** *licenses to buy certain drugs."*

To be 'cured' against one's will and cured of states which we may not regard as disease is to be put on a level with those who have not yet reached the age of reason or those who never will; to be classed with infants, imbeciles, and domestic animals."

Although at present we cannot serve the cause of liberty by repealing the drug laws, we can betray that cause by supporting the fiction that self-medication is a disease, prohibiting it is a public health measure, and punishing it is a treatment.

Legalizing Drugs Would Not Cause an Increase in Drug Use

by Dan Gardner

About the author: *Dan Gardner is an editorial writer for the* Ottawa Citizen.

There is no credible evidence that the criminal prohibition of drugs keeps drug use and abuse down. In fact, although it may seem counter-intuitive, experience from all over the world shows that drug use rises and falls with surprisingly little regard for the legal status of drugs.

Drug prohibition has not kept drug use down. Removing prohibition is unlikely, in itself, to cause drug use to rise. This suggestion might seem jarring. We have faith in the power of criminal law to shape behaviour.

But consider this statement by UN Secretary-General Kofi Annan in his introduction to the United Nation's 1997 World Drug Report: "Although the consumption of drugs has been a fact of life for centuries, addiction has mushroomed over the last five decades." Annan might have added that rates of drug use, not just addiction, have exploded over the last five decades. He might also have mentioned that drug prohibition became fully entrenched in international law and aggressively enforced about five decades ago.

The Unsettling Truth

The unsettling truth is that the most frightening jumps in drug use the world has seen have happened after the introduction—or escalation—of drug prohibition. In the United States, the country that invented prohibition, Richard Nixon coined the phrase "War on Drugs" in 1968. He backed up this rhetoric with major new spending on prohibition that launched the Drug Enforcement Administration (DEA) in 1973.

And drug use? It exploded like never before in American history. Between 1974 and 1982, cocaine use quadrupled. That growth peaked at the beginning of the 1980s and there has been a gradual decline in the use of many drugs—but not all—since then. But 30 years later, drug-use rates are still vastly higher than before Nixon declared war.

That pattern can be seen all over the world. In Canada, marijuana was banned in 1923. At the time, the weed was so little used in this country that anyone could have smoked a joint on the steps of most police stations. Despite anti-marijuana hysteria and an unforgiving attitude among law enforcers in those years, there were only 25 marijuana convictions up to 1946.

In 1962, when an even tougher marijuana law was passed, the drug was still little known. But immediately after the law passed—in the same year, in fact—marijuana use began to grow exponentially. Now, almost one in four Canadians has inhaled.

China's Struggle

China's struggle with opium addiction in the 19th century is often held up as a contrary example, a country where drug abuse soared during a period of legal availability. In fact, during much of the period in which China wrestled with opium, the Chinese government forbade the importation, sale or use of opium; dealers were executed and at least a few users had their top lip cut off to prevent further smoking.

But more importantly, throughout this era China suffered social, political and economic disintegration. These are fertile conditions for drug abuse. India, the source-country of much of the opium that entered China, is illustrative. India was the world's biggest producer of opium in the 19th century, yet a British Royal Commission investigating opium addiction in India reported in 1896 that "the use of opium in India resembles that of liquor in the West, rather than that of an undesirable substance."

Drugs Were Absurdly Available

Moreover, at the same time that China endured its problems with opium, drugs of all kinds, not just opium, were freely available in Canada, the United States, Britain and most other countries. In fact, drugs were absurdly available right up until they were banned early in the 20th century. They could be had over the counter, or in the mail.

They were advertised with outlandish claims of health benefits. They were added to medicines, quasi-medicinal syrups and cordials, and beverages such as Coca-Cola—often without the presence of the drug being mentioned on the label. Children were commonly given what are now considered dangerous street drugs.

"Drug use rises and falls with surprisingly little regard for the legal status of drugs."

One popular cough syrup promised it would "suit the palate of the most exacting adult or the most capricious child" thanks to its special ingredient:

heroin. Obviously, the potential for abuse was enormous. Yet Western countries did not suffer epidemics of addiction.

Many individuals became dependent users, to be sure. But historians agree that their numbers did not steadily rise. (And those who were addicted were generally able to continue their lives as they had lived them, unlike the walking dead in modern drug ghettoes, such as Vancouver's Downtown Eastside.)

States with higher rates of drug incarceration experience higher rates of drug use. Crude opium imports to the U.S., which grew throughout much of the second half of the 19th century, dropped almost by half over a 15-year period beginning in the mid-1890s. Opium was legal throughout that period, but growing awareness of the health risks it posed convinced people to avoid it.

Choosing Not to Use Drugs

Right up until drugs were banned in the early part of the 20th century, the overwhelming majority of people simply chose not to use drugs, or they took drugs in modest quantities that neither damaged their health nor led them to addiction. In 1905, a U.S. Congressional committee studied cocaine and opiate (opium, morphine and heroin) use and concluded there were some 200,000 dependant users in the United States. That's about 0.25 per cent of the population of the day.

"The most frightening jumps in drug use the world has seen have happened after the introduction—or escalation—of drug prohibition."

Other researchers put the number somewhat higher. David Musto, professor of history at Yale University, says there were "perhaps 250,000" addicts in the U.S.—or 0.3 per cent of the population.

How do those numbers compare to the U.S. today, after 84 years of fiercely enforced prohibition? In 1998, according to the U.S. government, there were 4,323,000 "hardcore" users (meaning they use these drugs at least weekly) of cocaine and heroin. That's about 1.6 per cent of the population—around six times the proportion at the beginning of the century.

The U.S. government considers about five million Americans to be hardcore users of any illegal drug. That's almost 1.8 per cent of the population. The numbers from early in the 20th century are little more than educated guesswork.

There are also serious problems with the modern figures—for one, they omit drug users among the two million prisoners in the U.S. and therefore seriously understate the reality; they also leave out the undoubtedly large number of people abusing prescription drugs such as Valium.

But taking these figures as broad indicators, they paint a startling picture: In the 20th century, when American drug policy went from extreme laissez-faire to extreme prohibition, the proportion of the population that abuses drugs dramatically increased.

Drug Punishments and Drug Use

Today, American states vary substantially in how readily they punish drug crimes with imprisonment. Some states are quite liberal; others have given life sentences for mere possession. If punishment is an effective deterrent, there should be more drug use in states with lighter punishments, less in states that punish drugs brutally.

But a study released in 2000 by the Justice Policy Institute, an American think tank, found a statistical correla-

> *"States with higher rates of drug incarceration experience higher rates of drug use."*

tion linking more severe drug punishments with more drug use. "States with higher rates of drug incarceration experience higher, not lower, rates of drug use," the report concluded.

The other American experiment in prohibition wasn't much more positive. In the decade before alcohol was banned in 1920, consumption dropped steadily. That drop continued for two years after Prohibition became law. Then consumption started to rise rapidly and would almost certainly have surpassed the pre-Prohibition level if alcohol hadn't been legalized in 1933.

This happened despite the fact that Prohibition pushed up the price of beer by 700 per cent and that of spirits by 270 per cent. Higher prices didn't make Americans give up the bottle, they only took more money from their pockets.

So there's little evidence that prohibition keeps drug use down. But what if we look at that question from the opposite direction? Once criminal prohibition is in place, would easing or lifting it cause greater drug use? Again, international experience says no.

The Australian state of South Australia decriminalized marijuana in 1987, and although there was some rise in marijuana use subsequently, it was no greater than that in two neighbouring states that didn't change their laws. The same thing happened in 11 American states that decriminalized marijuana in the 1970s. There were rises in use, but they were the same as in neighbouring states that didn't change their laws. (And when several of these states re-criminalized marijuana, this did not reduce consumption.)

In fact, American states with the most severe anti-marijuana laws experienced the sharpest rises in marijuana use.

Far from Exploding

Then there is the justly famous case of Holland. Marijuana possession was made de facto legal in 1976 and "coffee shops" selling marijuana under tightly regulated circumstances were permitted in 1980. When these policies were introduced, there was no increase in use.

There were, however, increases in use after 1984, but equal or greater increases occurred in the U.S., Britain and many other countries that stuck with criminal prohibition. The Dutch rate of marijuana use continues to be one of the lowest in the western world. Holland also made the possession of small amounts of other drugs, including heroin and cocaine, de facto legal.

Yet Dutch consumption of these drugs, far from exploding when the criminal law was pulled back, stayed fairly stable. Methodologically rigorous surveys of international drug usage rates haven't been done, but most Western countries do have good domestic research whose outlines provide grounds for broad comparisons.

These comparisons show the Dutch use of illegal drugs is far lower than in the U.S. The Dutch rate of heroin addiction is a fraction of that in the U.S., and is lower than in most European countries. The Dutch rate of drug-related deaths is the lowest in Europe, leading to a uniquely Dutch problem: finding housing for senior-citizen addicts.

Toward Decriminalization

Not surprisingly, many European countries are now moving toward the decriminalization or de facto legalization of mere possession of drugs. Some states and cities in Germany chose this policy in the early 1990s. Italy and Spain have formally adopted this approach.

Critics in each case insisted drug use would soar, and in each case it didn't happen. Impressed by these results, Portugal voted in July 2000 to follow suit. Obviously these facts do not mean that liberalized drug laws "cause" lower rates of drug use.

Culture, not law and government policy, is the crucial factor in pushing use up or down. But the data show that removing the criminal ban on drugs will not in itself cause drug use and addiction to soar. It's not hard to understand why: People can think for themselves. They can make rational choices and, since most people are not self-destructive, they usually do. That's something prohibition's supporters too often ignore.

Eugene Oscapella, an Ottawa lawyer and a director of the Canadian Foundation for Drug Policy, notes that "we can all go out right now and get ourselves totally blotto on any number of legal drugs but the vast majority of us don't do that. We have our own internal control mechanisms. So the fact that a drug is going to be decriminalized or regulated in a way that is different than now and the price may fall doesn't mean there's going to be an explosion in use. Not by any means."

Mindless Impulses?

The very fact that a great majority of Canadians want drugs to be criminally prohibited is a good indication that they personally don't want to use them. Would these people suddenly want to shoot heroin or snort cocaine if the legal status of these drugs changed? I've put that question to many people who passionately disagree with legalization but I've never met anyone who answered yes.

So who is it that will start using drugs if they're no longer banned by criminal law? It's not you, of course. And it's not me. It's those other people—the masses who have to be protected from their own mindless impulses.

"It all depends on what you believe of society," says Oscapella. "Are we just a bunch of uncontrolled people who need the criminal law to go ahead and dictate our behaviours?" For prohibition to make sense, that bleak view of humanity is exactly what you have to believe.

The evidence, happily, does not support that belief. It's clear that our fellow men and women are capable of making intelligent decisions about their own lives. Perhaps we might put a little more trust in them, and a lot less in criminal law.

Harm Reduction Reduces the Risks of Drug Use

by Herbert P. Barnard

About the author: *Herbert P. Barnard is a counselor for health and welfare at the Royal Netherlands Embassy.*

Drug use is a fact of life and needs to be discouraged in as practical a manner as possible.

"The Dutch policy on drugs is a disastrous mistake. The Netherlands regrets its liberal policy and is about to turn back the clock." "Drug use has increased by 250 percent in two years, armed robberies by 70 percent, shoot-outs by 40 percent, and car thefts by 60 percent." "In the Netherlands, 1,600 addicts receive daily injections of heroin on government orders." "In Amsterdam recently, a father who was addicted to cannabis massacred his whole family." "There's plenty of heroin for sale in every Dutch coffee shop."

Do you believe all this? I am quoting just a few statements by foreign politicians and other "experts" who disagree with the Netherlands' drug policy. There is evidently an audience willing to believe all this, which gives such critics a reason to continue spreading these stories. Aside from questioning the honesty of this approach, one should ask what purpose is served by repeating such nonsense. It is certainly not in the interest of drug users, their immediate neighbors, the government, or health-care and social service institutions.

The drug problem is too serious an issue to be used as a political football by ambitious politicians. Nor should it be the subject of speculations about reality, making the facts of the matter irrelevant. As a representative of the Netherlands government, I take this opportunity to present the facts.

Individual Freedom

To understand the Dutch drug policy, you need to know a little about the Netherlands and the Dutch people. After all, a country's drug policy has to fit in with the nation's characteristics and culture.

From "The Netherlands' Drug Policy: 20 Years of Experience," by Herbert P. Barnard, *The World & I*, October 1, 1998.

The Netherlands is one of the most densely populated countries in the world, with around 15.5 million people in an area one-quarter the size of New York State. Commerce and transport have traditionally been important sectors of industry in our country. Rotterdam is the busiest port in the world, handling almost 5 million containers a year. In fact, the Netherlands is generally seen as the gateway to Europe.

The Dutch have a strong belief in individual freedom. Government is expected to avoid becoming involved in matters of morality and religion. At the same time, we feel a strong sense of responsibility for the well-being of the community. The Netherlands has a very extensive system of social security, while health care and education are accessible to everyone.

What is the Dutch drug policy? The main objective is to minimize the risks associated with drug use, both for users themselves and those around them. This objective was formulated in the mid-1970s. . . .

Many elements of the harm-reduction approach are very similar to Dutch drug policy. Our policy does not moralize but is based on the idea that drug use is a fact of life and needs to be discouraged in as practical a manner as possible. This calls for a pragmatic and flexible approach that recognizes the risks for both drug users and those around them.

Reducing Demand and Supply

Our policy focuses on reducing demand as well as supply. A combination of these two instruments requires close cooperation with public health and law enforcement authorities on all policy levels. Furthermore, we invest a lot of money in cure and prevention. Since the 1970s and early '80s, respectively, low-threshold methadone provision and needle exchange programs have been important elements in our harm-reduction approach.

Our policy is based on two important principles. The first is the distinction between types of drugs, based on their harmfulness (hemp products on the one hand and drugs with unacceptable risks on the other). The second legal principle is a differentiation according to the nature of the punishable acts, such as the distinction between the possession of small quantities of drugs for one's own use and possession with intent to deal. This makes it possible to pursue a finely tuned policy based on the application of criminal law.

The possession of up to 30 grams of cannabis is a petty offense punishable with a fine. The sale of small amounts of cannabis, through what are known as "coffee shops," subject to strict conditions, is not prosecuted. The idea behind the policy on coffee shops is that of "separating the markets." The reasoning is that if retailers of cannabis

> *"What is the Dutch drug policy? The main objective is to minimize the risks associated with drug use, both for users themselves and those around them."*

are not prosecuted under certain conditions, the experimenting user will not be forced to move in criminal circles, where higher profits are made by urging users to take more dangerous drugs (such as heroin).

People often think that drugs are available legally in the Netherlands and that we do not focus on combating the supply side of the drug market. Nothing could be less true. Aside from the retail trade in cannabis, a high priority is given to tackling all other forms of drug dealing. The police and customs authorities seize large consignments of drugs almost every week, working closely with other countries in the fight against organized crime.

Not Legalization in Disguise

Some people think that harm reduction and legalization are synonymous. I disagree and would like to emphasize that harm reduction is not legalization in disguise. Harm reduction is first and foremost concerned with reducing the risks and hazards of drug taking. Harm reduction is meant to reduce the risks for not only the drug user but the immediate environment (i.e., the public) and society as well. This implies that intensive cooperation at all times between those providing care for addicts, the criminal justice authorities, and the government is an essential element in the harm reduction approach.

"People often think that . . . we do not focus on combating the supply side of the drug market. Nothing could be less true."

What are the results of our policy? The Dutch government recently issued a document discussing its drug policy, evaluating the policy of the last 20 years, and mapping out approaches for the future. This paper can be compared with the yearly National Drug Control Strategies of the White House Office of National Drug Control Policy. I will summarize the main outcomes.

Regarding the evaluation of Dutch policy on hard drugs, the document makes the following points:

Our policy of harm reduction has been quite successful. Thanks to a high standard of care and prevention, including extensive low-level and nonconditional methadone prescription, social and medical assistance for drug users, and a large-scale free needle-exchange program, we have reached a situation that is matched by few other countries.

The number of addicts in the Netherlands is relatively low compared with that in many countries. This implies that harm-reduction measures do not increase the use of drugs.

The population of addicts is rather stable and rapidly aging. This suggests that few new users are joining in. Heroin is not fashionable among youngsters. The average age of Amsterdam methadone-provision clients increases by almost one year every year, and the number of young heroin users using services like methadone provision has shrunk over the years to a handful. The average

age of Amsterdam methadone-provision clients was 36.2 years in 1995. The average age of newly registered drug clients in the Netherlands was 32 years in 1995.

The mortality rate among drug users is low, due to the low-threshold methadone programs that provide protection against overdose.

The damage to health caused by the use of hard drugs has been kept within limits. The number of addicts infected with HIV is exceptionally low. In the Netherlands, the percentage of intravenous drug users (IDUs) among the total cumulative number of AIDS

> *"Harm-reduction measures do not increase the use of drugs."*

cases is low. In addition, the incidence of HIV infections among IDUs has decreased since 1986. An evaluation study concluded that a combination of harm-reduction measures (i.e., methadone provision, needle exchange, training, and counseling) has resulted in safer sexual and drug-taking behaviors. Safe sex practices among addicted prostitutes have increased as well.

Another result of our policy is that a comparatively large proportion of drug users in our country has been integrated into society to a reasonable extent.

A Tolerant Policy

The number of regular hemp smokers has gradually increased in recent years. Lifetime prevalence and last-month prevalence have increased substantially since 1984. An annual survey among older pupils in Amsterdam showed, however, that the prevalence of cannabis use has stabilized since 1993–94. This might indicate that we have reached the peak of the upward trend of the past years.

Can the increase in cannabis use, especially among students, be attributed to the existence of coffee shops in the Netherlands? An analysis of surveys shows an upward trend in many other European countries. Since the late 1980s, cannabis use among youngsters (as well as the general population) has increased in France, the United Kingdom, Germany, and the United States.

Compared with the U.S. prevalence, the figures for the Netherlands are considerably lower. According to the results of the 1995 Monitoring the Future Surveys, published by the University of Michigan, cannabis use has increased tremendously among American youngsters. To my knowledge, this increase cannot be attributed to any significant change of policy.

The fact that the rate of cannabis use in the Netherlands is comparable with that in other countries (and even lower than in the United States) shows that government policy probably has less influence on use than we think. Other factors, such as trends in youth culture, social differences, and other social influences, probably play a far more important role. In our view, this does not mean that it makes no difference whether one pursues a liberal or a restrictive drug policy. The difference is that a tolerant policy prevents the marginalization of the user. A situation often encountered in other nations, where the user—in most cases a minor—runs the risk of getting into trouble with the police, is seen as highly undesirable in my country.

A Serious Effort

Some conclusions:

1. Comparisons with other countries show no indications that our policy has led to an increase in the number of cannabis users. Therefore, there is no reason to change our policy on cannabis.

2. Our policy on cannabis has not led to an increase in the number of hard-drug users. In the Netherlands, the stepping-stone hypothesis cannot be confirmed.

3. The wide range of provisions for care and prevention has held down the number of hard-drug users, and has ensured that the health of these users can be described as reasonable. Harm reduction actually works, if you invest in it.

4. By definition, the Dutch drug policy requires an integral cooperation with public health, law enforcement, and public order officials.

The Dutch drug policy, therefore, is not a disastrous experiment but a serious effort to tackle a serious issue. Our policy has produced results that are demonstrably better than those in many of the countries criticizing us. While we realize that an ongoing dialogue with all those involved with the drug problem is a precondition for any progress, we are not going to change our policy on the basis of unjustified criticism.

Drug Use Should Not Be Legalized

by Donnie Marshall

About the author: *Donnie Marshall is deputy administrator of the Drug Enforcement Administration (DEA).*

Whether all drugs are eventually legalized or not, the practical outcome of legalizing even one, like marijuana, is to increase the amount of usage among all drugs. It's been said that you can't put the genie back in the bottle or the toothpaste back in the tube. I think those are apt metaphors for what will happen if America goes down the path of legalization. Once America gives into a drug culture, and all the social decay that comes with such a culture, it would be very hard to restore a decent civic culture without a cost to America's civil liberties that would be prohibitively high.

There is a huge amount of research about drugs and their effect on society, here and abroad. I'll let others better acquainted with all of the scholarly literature discuss that research. What I will do is suggest four probable outcomes of legalization and then make a case why a policy of drug enforcement works.

Legalization Would Boost Drug Use

The first outcome of legalization would be to have a lot more drugs around, and, in turn, a lot more drug abuse. I can't imagine anyone arguing that legalizing drugs would reduce the amount of drug abuse we already have. Although drug use is down from its high mark in the late 1970s, America still has entirely too many people who are on drugs.

In 1962, for example, only four million Americans had ever tried a drug in their entire lifetime. In 1997, the latest year for which we have figures, 77 million Americans had tried drugs. Roughly half of all high school seniors have tried drugs by the time they graduate.

The result of having a lot of drugs around and available is more and more consumption. To put it another way, supply to some degree drives demand. That is

Excerpted from Donnie Marshall's testimony before the United States House of Representatives, House Committee on Government Reform, Subcommittee on Criminal Justice, Drug Policy, and Human Resources, June 16, 1999.

an outcome that has been apparent from the early days of drug enforcement.

What legalization could mean for drug consumption in the United States can be seen in the drug liberalization experiment in Holland. In 1976, Holland decided to liberalize its laws regarding marijuana. Since then, Holland has acquired a reputation as the drug capital of Europe. For example, a majority of the synthetic drugs, such as Ecstasy (MDMA) and methamphetamine, now used in the United Kingdom are produced in Holland.

Creating a Market

The effect of supply on demand can also be seen even in countries that take a tougher line on drug abuse. An example is the recent surge in heroin use in the United States. In the early 1990s, cocaine traffickers from Colombia discovered that there was a lot more profit with a lot less work in selling heroin. Several years ago, they began to send heroin from South America to the United States.

To make as much money as possible, they realized they needed not only to respond to a market, but also to create a market. They devised an aggressive marketing campaign which included the use of brand names and the distribution of free samples of heroin to users who bought their cocaine. In many cases, they induced distributors to move quantities of heroin to stimulate market growth. The traffickers greatly increased purity levels, allowing many potential addicts who might be squeamish about using needles to inhale the heroin rather than injecting it. The result has been a huge increase in the number of people trying heroin for the first time, five times as many in 1997 as just four years before.

I don't mean to imply that demand is not a critical factor in the equation. But any informed drug policy should take into consideration that supply has a great influence on demand. In 1997, American companies spent $73 billion advertising their products and services. These advertisers certainly must have a well-documented reason to believe that consumers are susceptible to the power of suggestion, or they wouldn't be spending all that money. The market for drugs is no different. International drug traffickers are spending enormous amounts of money to make sure that drugs are available to every American kid in a school yard.

Dr. Herbert Kleber, a professor of psychiatry at Columbia University College of Physicians and Surgeons, and one of the nation's leading authorities on addiction, stated in a 1994 article in the *New England Journal of Medicine* that clinical data support the premise that drug use would increase with legalization. He said: "There are over 50 million nicotine addicts, 18 million alcoholics or problem drinkers, and fewer than 2 million cocaine addicts in the United States. Cocaine is a much more addictive drug than alcohol. If cocaine were legally available, as alcohol and nicotine are now, the number

"The first outcome of legalization would be to have a lot more drugs around, and, in turn, a lot more drug abuse."

of cocaine abusers would probably rise to a point somewhere between the number of users of the other two agents, perhaps 20 to 25 million . . . the number of compulsive users might be nine times higher than the current number. When drugs have been widely available—as . . . cocaine was at the turn of the century—both use and addiction have risen."

Contributing to a Rise in Crime

I can't imagine the impact on this society if that many people were abusers of cocaine. From what we know about the connection between drugs and crime, America would certainly have to devote an enormous amount of its financial resources to law enforcement.

The second outcome of legalization would be more crime, especially more violent crime. There's a close relationship between drugs and crime. This relationship is borne out by the statistics. Every year, the Justice Department compiles a survey of people arrested in a number of American cities to determine how many of them tested positive for drugs at the time of their arrest. In 1998, the survey found, for example, that 74 percent of those arrested in Atlanta for a violent crime tested positive for drugs. In Miami, 49 percent; in Oklahoma City, 60 percent.

There's a misconception that most drug-related crimes involve people who are looking for money to buy drugs. The fact is that the most drug-

"There's a close relationship between drugs and crime."

related crimes are committed by people under the influence of mind-altering drugs. A 1994 study by the Bureau of Justice Statistics compared Federal and state prison inmates in 1991. It found that 18 percent of the Federal inmates incarcerated for homicide had committed homicide under the influence of drugs, whereas 2.7 percent of these individuals had committed the offense to obtain money to buy drugs. The same disparities showed up for state inmates: almost 28 percent committed homicide under the influence versus 5.3 percent to obtain the money to buy drugs.

Under the Influence

Those who propose legalization argue that it would cut down on the number of drug-related crimes because addicts would no longer need to rob people to buy their drugs from illicit sources. But even supposing that argument is true, which I don't think that it is, the fact is that so many more people would be abusing drugs, and committing crimes under the influence of drugs, that the crime rate would surely go up rather than down.

It's clear that drugs often cause people to do things they wouldn't do if they were drug-free. Too many drug users lose the kind of self-control and common sense that keeps them in bounds. In 1998, in the small community of Albion, Illinois, two young men went on a widely reported, one-week, non-stop binge on methamphetamine. At the end of it, they started a killing rampage that left five people dead. One was a Mennonite farmer. They shot him as he was working in his fields. Another was a mother of four. They hijacked her car and killed her. . . .

Consequences for Society

The third outcome of legalization would be a far different social environment. The social cost of drug abuse is not found solely in the amount of crime it causes. Drugs cause an enormous amount of accidents, domestic violence, illness, and lost opportunities for many who might have led happy, productive lives.

Drug abuse takes a terrible toll on the health and welfare of a lot of American families. In 1996, for example, there were almost 15,000 drug-induced deaths in the United States, and a half-million emergency room episodes related to drugs. The Centers for Disease Control and Prevention has estimated that 36 percent of new HIV cases are directly or indirectly linked to injecting drug users.

Increasing drug use has had a major impact on the workplace. According to estimates in the 1997 National Household Survey, a study conducted by the Substance Abuse and Mental Health Services Administration (SAMHSA), 6.7 million full-time workers and 1.6 million part-time workers are current users of illegal drugs.

Public Safety Risks

Employees who test positive for drug use consume almost twice the medical benefits as nonusers, are absent from work 50 percent more often, and make more than twice as many workers' compensation claims. Drug use also presents an enormous safety problem in the workplace.

This is particularly true in the transportation sector. Marijuana, for example, impairs the ability of drivers to maintain concentration and show good judgment on the road. A study released by the National Institute on Drug Abuse surveyed 6,000 teenage drivers. It studied those who drove more than six times a month after using marijuana. The study found that they were about two-and-a-half times more likely to be involved in a traffic accident than those who didn't smoke marijuana before driving.

The problem is compounded when drivers have the additional responsibility for the safety of many lives. . . .

In addition to these public safety risks and the human misery costs to drug users and their families associated with drug abuse, the Office of National Drug Control Policy has put a financial price tag on this social ill. According to the 1999 National Drug Control Strategy, illegal drugs cost society about $110 billion every year.

Proponents of legalization point to several liberalization experiments in Europe for example, the one in Holland that I have already mentioned. The experiment in Holland [started in 1976], so it provides a good illustration of what liberalizing our drug laws portends.

The Drug Culture

The head of Holland's best known drug abuse rehabilitation center has described what the new drug culture has created. The strong form of marijuana that most of the young people smoke, he says, produces "a chronically passive individual. . . . someone who is lazy, who doesn't want to take initiatives, doesn't want to be active—the kid who'd prefer to lie in bed with a joint in the morning rather than getting up and doing something."

England's experience with widely available heroin shows that use and addiction increase. In a policy far more liberal than America's, Great Britain allowed doctors to prescribe heroin to addicts. There was an explosion of heroin use. According to James Q. Wilson, in 1960, there were 68 heroin addicts registered with the British Government. Today, there are roughly 31,000.

Liberalization in Switzerland has had much the same results. This small nation became a magnet for drug users the world over. In 1987, Zurich permitted drug use and sales in a part of the city called Platzspitz, dubbed "Needle Park." By 1992 the number of regular drug users at the park had reportedly swelled from a few hundred in 1982 to 21,000 by 1992. The experiment has since been terminated.

Increasing Our Problems

In April, 1994, a number of European cities signed a resolution titled "European Cities Against Drugs," commonly known as the Stockholm resolution. Currently the signatories include 184 cities or municipalities in 30 different countries in Europe. As the resolution stated: . . . the answer does not lie in making harmful drugs more accessible, cheaper and socially acceptable. Attempts to do this have not proved successful. We believe that legalizing drugs will, in the long term, increase our problems. By making them legal, society will signal that it has resigned to the acceptance of drug abuse." I couldn't say it any better than that. After seeing the results of liberalization up close, these European cities clearly believe that liberalization is a bad idea.

You do not have to visit Amsterdam or Zurich or London to witness the effects of drug abuse. If you really want to discover what legalization might mean for society, talk to a local clergyman or an eighth grade teacher, or a high school coach, or a scout leader or a parent. How many teachers do you know who come and visit your offices and say, Congressman, the thing that our kids need more than anything else is greater availability to drugs. How many parents have you ever known to say, "I sure wish my child could find illegal drugs more easily than he can now"? . . .

> *"Most drug-related crimes are committed by people under the influence of mind-altering drugs."*

A Law Enforcement Nightmare

The fourth outcome of legalization would be a law enforcement nightmare. I suspect few people would want to make drugs available to 12-year-old children. That reluctance points to a major flaw in the legalization proposal. Drugs will always be denied to some sector of the population, so there will always be some form of black market and a need for drug enforcement.

Consider some of the questions that legalization raises: What drugs will be legalized? Will it be limited to marijuana? What is a safe dosage of methamphetamine or of crack cocaine? If the principle is advanced that drug abuse is a victimless crime, why limit drug use to marijuana?

> *"Drugs cause an enormous amount of accidents, domestic violence, illness, and lost opportunities for many who might have led happy, productive lives."*

I know that there are those who will make the case that drug addiction hurts no one but the user. If that becomes falsely part of the conventional wisdom, there will certainly be pressure to legalize all drug use. Only when people come to realize how profoundly all of us are affected by widespread drug abuse will there be pressure to put the genie back in the bottle. By then, it may be too late.

But deciding what drugs to legalize will only be part of the problem. Who will be able to buy drugs legally? Only those over 18 or 21? If so, you can bet that many young people who have reached the legal age will divert their supplies to younger friends. Of course, these young pushers will be in competition with many of the same people who are now pushing drugs in school yards and neighborhood streets.

Any attempt to limit drug use to any age group at all will create a black market, with all of the attendant crime and violence, thereby defeating one of the goals purported of legalization. That's also true if legalization is limited to marijuana. Cocaine, heroin and methamphetamine will be far more profitable products for the drug lords. Legalization of marijuana alone would do little to stem illegal trafficking.

A Right to Drugs?

Will airline pilots be able to use drugs? Heart surgeons? People in law enforcement or the military? Teachers? Pregnant women? Truck drivers? Workers in potentially dangerous jobs like construction?

Drug use has been demonstrated to result in lower work-place productivity, and often ends in serious, life-threatening accidents. Many drug users are so debilitated by their habit that they can't hold jobs. Which raises the question, if drug users can't hold a job, where will they get the money to buy drugs? Will the right to use drugs imply a right to the access to drugs? If so, who will distribute free drugs? Government employees? The local supermarket? The college bookstore? If they can't hold a job, who will provide their food, clothing and shelter?

Virtually any form of legalization will create a patchwork quilt of drug laws and drug enforcement. The confusion would swamp our precinct houses and courtrooms. I don't think it would be possible to effectively enforce the remaining drug laws in that kind of environment.

Drug Enforcement Works

This is no time to undermine America's effort to stem drug abuse. America's drug policies work. From 1979 to 1994, the number of drug users in America dropped by almost half. Two things significantly contributed to that outcome. First, a strong program of public education; second, a strict program of law enforcement.

If you look over the last four decades, you can see a pattern develop. An independent researcher, R.E. Peterson, has analyzed this period, using statistics from a wide variety of sources, including the Justice Department and the White House Office of National Drug Control Strategy. He broke these four decades down into two periods: the first, from 1960 to 1980, an era of permissive drug laws; the second, from 1980 to 1995, an era of tough drug laws.

During the permissive period, drug incarceration rates fell almost 80 percent. During the era of tough drug laws, drug incarceration rates rose al-

> *"Employees who test positive for drug use . . . are absent for work 50 percent more often."*

most 450 percent. Just as you might expect, these two policies regarding drug abuse had far different consequences. During the permissive period, drug use among teens climbed by more than 500 percent. During the tough era, drug use by high school students dropped by more than a third.

Is there an absolute one-to-one correlation between tougher drug enforcement and a declining rate of drug use? I wouldn't suggest that. But the contrasts of drug abuse rates between the two eras of drug enforcement are striking. . . .

In fact, the history of America's experience with drugs has shown us that it was strong drug enforcement that effectively ended America's first drug epidemic, which lasted from the mid-1880s to the mid-1920s.

By 1923, about half of all prisoners at the Federal penitentiary in Leavenworth, Kansas, were violators of America's first drug legislation, the Harrison Act. If you are concerned by the high drug incarceration rates of the late 1990s, consider the parallels to the tough drug enforcement policies of the 1920s. It was those tough policies that did much to create America's virtually drug-free environment of the mid-20th Century.

Drug laws can work, if we have the national resolve to enforce them. As a father, as someone who's had a lot of involvement with the Boy Scouts and Little

Leaguers, and as a 30-year civil servant in drug enforcement, I can tell you that there are a lot of young people out there looking for help. . . .

Helping Young People

America spends millions of dollars every year on researching the issue of drugs. We have crime statistics and opinion surveys and biochemical research. And all of that is important. But what it all comes down to is whether we can help young people . . . whether we can keep them from taking that first step into the world of drugs that will ruin their careers, destroy their marriages and leave them in a cycle of dependency on chemicals.

Whether in rural areas, in the suburbs, or in the inner cities, there are a lot of kids who could use a little help. Sometimes that help can take the form of education and counseling. Often it takes a stronger approach. And there are plenty of young people, and older people as well, who could use it.

If we as a society are unwilling to have the courage to say no to drug abuse, we will find that drugs will not only destroy the society we have built up over 200 years, but ruin millions of young people. . . .

Drug abuse, and the crime and personal dissolution and social decay that go with it, is not inevitable. Too many people in America seem resigned to the growing rates of drug use. But America's experience with drugs shows that strong law enforcement policies can and do work.

At DEA, our mission is to fight drug trafficking in order to make drug abuse expensive, unpleasant, risky, and disreputable. If drug users aren't worried about their health, or the health and welfare of those who depend on them, they should at least worry about the likelihood of getting caught.

Marijuana Should Not Be Legalized

by Bob Barr

About the author: *Bob Barr, a former attorney, is a U.S. Representative from the seventh district of Georgia and serves on the House Judiciary Committee.*

In 1998, as the Reagan presidency and its successful "Just Say No" campaign were coming to a close, drug legalization advocates decided it was time for a change in tactics. With drug abuse rates actually dropping for the first time since the drug revolution began, and a White House strongly committed to fighting mind-altering drugs, the legalization movement faced a choice: become irrelevant, or camouflage its true goals in order to move its agenda forward. The movement chose for its disguise "Medical" marijuana.

As UCLA Public Policy Professor Mark Kleiman told the *New York Times* in June 1999, "[m]edical marijuana was chosen as a wedge issue several years ago by people who wanted to move drug policy in a softer direction."

In other words, the true aim of medicinal marijuana advocates is not to put drugs in the hands of doctors and pharmacists. Rather, the goal is to make marijuana and other drugs widely and legally available. To them, the medicinal-use argument is simply a contrived means to an end; using terminally ill patients as pawns in a cynical political game.

A Political Standpoint

From a purely political standpoint, the medicinal strategy has worked rather well for the legalizers. Backed by a handful of wealthy patrons like George Soros, in a few short years legalization advocates have transformed themselves from socially unacceptable pariahs into the darlings of the national media. News reports on marijuana protestors at rallies became magically changed—with a speed that would make Cinderella green with envy—into stories about a repressive government denying "life-saving" drugs to "patients."

Putting the intellectual dishonesty of the legalization movement aside for a

From "Marijuana Should Not Be Legalized, Under Any Pretense," by Bob Barr, *The Commonwealth*, June 1999. Copyright © 1999 by Bob Barr. Reprinted with permission.

moment, let's take a look at the medicinal use argument on its own merits, or lack thereof.

THC, the active ingredient in smoked marijuana, has been a legal prescription drug (marinol) available in the United States since 1984. For over a decade, physicians have been able to prescribe the active ingredient in marijuana. However, they rarely do, because other remedies—including drugs as well as medically-supervised pain management techniques—provide its therapeutic qualities more effectively. No reputable study has arrived at the conclusion that smoked marijuana has any therapeutic value sufficient to justify its medicinal use.

Harmful, If Not Deadly

Not only is there no real proof that marijuana has any significant medicinal value, there is voluminous evidence that it is demonstrably harmful, if not deadly. For example, marijuana smoke contains roughly 30 times as many carcinogens as cigarette smoke. It is also dangerously addictive. Nationally, an estimated 100,000 individuals are in treatment for marijuana use.

Furthermore, inhalation of marijuana smoke depresses the immune system. This makes it likely that allowing its use by those with weak immune systems, such as AIDS patients, would be highly questionable at best, and harmful at worst. Surely, well-informed observers would condemn a movement that fills the terminally ill with false hope, and encourages patients already vulnerable to pulmonary infections and tumors like Kaposi's sarcoma, to put a deadly substance in their lungs.

Moreover, marijuana use adversely affects the user's memory; a fact patently obvious in debates involving heavy marijuana users.

A Threat to All of Us

Marijuana use poses an even greater danger from a sociological standpoint than it does to the health of individuals who smoke it. Numerous studies have indicated marijuana use leads to abuse of other drugs like heroin, LSD, and cocaine. Using data compiled by the Centers for Disease Control, researchers at Columbia University—hardly a bastion of conservative thought—concluded that children who drank, smoked cigarettes, or used marijuana at least once in the past month, were 16 times as likely to use another drug like cocaine, heroin, or LSD.

> *"The true aim of medicinal marijuana advocates is not to put drugs in the hands of doctors and pharmacists."*

At the workplace, marijuana is a proven cause of absenteeism, accidents, and increased insurance claims. Estimates put the annual cost of on the job drug use at more than $100 billion per year.

On America's roads, marijuana poses a threat to all of us. Unlike alcohol, it is difficult to use roadside tests to determine the extent to which a driver is under the influence of marijuana, and there is practically no way for law enforcement to determine to what degree a particular driver's perception is altered by the drug; though by definition perception is altered (marijuana is a mind-altering drug for that reason). A recent study of reckless drivers found that 45% of those drivers not under the influence of alcohol tested positive for marijuana.

California has made national headlines by embarking on an obsessive campaign to eradicate cigarette smoking from public places. Ironically, in the same period, the state voted in favor of widely distributing a substance 30 times deadlier. What an imminently logical approach. What's next? Legalizing DDT and banning fly-swatters?

Ignore Science?

Proponents of allowing doctors to dispense marijuana frequently make the simplistic, but media-friendly, argument that doctors, not the government, should decide what drugs to prescribe. Accepting this premise, why have an FDA approval process at all? Why not just return to the 19th century, when "doctors" could prescribe any remedy—from powdered rhinoceros horn to sugar water in medicine bottles—that they personally felt was efficacious? Who needs science? Why not just ignore science, shut down the FDA, get rid of pharmacists, and stock pharmacy shelves by voter referendum?

Where else would medicinal legalization lead us? Undoubtedly, high school students—backed by the ACLU—would begin filing and winning lawsuits for permission to smoke their "medicine" in class, under a perverse interpretation of the equal protection clause of the Constitution. Others, from prisoners to bus drivers, would assuredly do the same. Medicinal use would create a nightmare for employers. Accidents would increase, and employers could no longer test workers for drug use, for fear of winding up in court. Adding insult to injury, companies would be forced to pay for workers to get stoned on the job by including marijuana "treatment" in health plans. Everyone who drives a car would also be forced to foot the bill for this folly, in the form of increased accidents and higher insurance rates.

The Bottom Line

The bottom line is that legalization advocates don't care about any of these things. They are motivated either by a simple desire to smoke dope because it makes them feel good, or a misguided political philosophy that tells them legalizing drugs would end crime with one magical puff of smoke.

Unfortunately, citizens of several states have been all too eager to buy the snake oil legalizers are selling, because it is tantalizingly packaged in fake compassion and false hope for the sick. Hopefully, voters in other states will take the time to carefully consider the facts before they make an ill-formed decision to follow California's example.

Harm Reduction Does Not Reduce the Risks of Drug Use

by Barry R. McCaffrey

About the author: *Barry R. McCaffrey is the former director of the Office of National Drug Control Safety.*

The so-called harm-reduction approach to drugs confuses people with terminology. All drug policies claim to reduce harm. No reasonable person advocates a position consciously designed to be harmful. The real question is which policies actually decrease harm and increase good. The approach advocated by people who say they favor harm reduction would in fact harm Americans.

The theory behind what they call harm reduction is that illegal drugs cannot be controlled by law enforcement, education and other methods; therefore, proponents say, harm should be reduced by needle exchange, decriminalization of drugs, heroin maintenance and other measures. But the real intent of many harm reduction advocates is the legalization of drugs, which would be a mistake.

Favoring Drug Legalization

Lest anyone question whether harm reductionists favor drug legalization, let me quote some articles written by supporters of this position. Ethan Nadelmann, director of the Lindesmith Center, a Manhattan-based drug research institute, wrote in *American Heritage* (March, 1993): "Should we legalize drugs? History answers 'yes.'" In *Issues in Science and Technology* (June, 1990), Nadelmann aligns his own opinion with history's supposed verdict: "Personally, when I talk about legalization, I mean three things: The first is to make drugs such as marijuana, cocaine and heroin legal." With regard to labels, Nadelmann wrote: "I much prefer the term 'decriminalization' or 'normalization.'"

People who advocate legalization can call themselves anything they like, but deceptive terms should not obscure a position so that it can't be debated coher-

From "Legalization Would Be the Wrong Decision" by Barry R. McCaffrey, *Los Angeles Times*, July 27, 1998.

ently. Changing the name of a plan doesn't constitute a new solution or alter the nature of the problem.

The plain fact is that drug abuse wrecks lives. It is criminal that more money is spent on illegal drugs than on art or higher education, that crack babies are born addicted and in pain and that thousands of adolescents lose their health and future to drugs.

Addictive drugs were criminalized because they are harmful; they are not harmful because they were criminalized. The more a product is available and legitimized, the greater will be its use. If drugs were legalized in the U.S., the cost to the individual and society would grow astronomically. In the Netherlands when coffee shops started selling marijuana in small quantities, use of this drug doubled between 1984 and 1992. A 1997 study by Robert MacCoun and Peter Reuter from the University of Maryland notes that the percentage of Dutch 18-year-olds who tried pot rose from 15% to 34% from 1984 to 1992, a time when the numbers weren't climbing in other European nations. By contrast, in 1992 teenage use of marijuana in the United States was estimated at 10.6%.

Toward the Absurd

Many advocates of harm reduction consider drug use a part of the human condition that will always be with us. While we agree that murder, pedophilia and child prostitution can never be eliminated entirely, no one is arguing that we legalize these activities.

Some measures proposed by activist harm reductionists, like heroin maintenance, veer toward the absurd. The Lindesmith Center convened a meeting in June 1998 to discuss a multicity heroin maintenance study, and a test program for heroin maintenance may be launched in Baltimore. Arnold Trebach argues for heroin maintenance in his book *Legalize It? Debating American Drug Policy*: "Under the legalization plan I propose here, addicts . . . would be able to purchase the heroin and needles they need at reasonable prices from a nonmedical drugstore."

Why would anyone choose to maintain addicts on heroin as opposed to oral methadone, which eliminates the injection route associated with HIV and other diseases? Research from the National Institute for Drug Abuse shows that untreated addicts die at a rate seven to eight times higher than similar patients in methadone-based treatment programs.

> *"The approach advocated by people who say they favor harm reduction would in fact harm Americans."*

Dr. Avram Goldstein, in his book *Addiction: From Biology to Drug Policy,* explains that when individuals switch from heroin to methadone, general health improves and abnormalities of body systems (such as the hormones) normalize. Unlike heroin maintenance, methadone maintenance has no adverse effects on cognitive or psychomotor function, performance of skilled tasks or memory, he said. This research indicates that the choice of heroin maintenance over methadone maintenance doesn't even meet the criteria of harm reduction that advocates claim to apply.

> *"The real intent of many harm reduction advocates is the legalization of drugs, which would be a mistake."*

Treatment must differ significantly from the disease it seeks to cure. Otherwise, the solution resembles the circular reasoning spoofed in Saint-Exupery's *The Little Prince* by the character who drinks because he has a terrible problem, namely, that he is a drunk. Just as alcohol is no help for alcoholism, heroin is no cure for heroin addiction.

As a society, we are successfully addressing drug use and its consequences. In the past 20 years, drug use in the United States decreased by half and casual cocaine use by 70%. Drug-related murders and spending on drugs decreased by more than 30% as the illegal drug market shrunk.

A Half-Way Measure

Still, we are faced with many challenges, including educating a new generation of children who may have little experience with the negative consequences of drug abuse, increasing access to treatment for 4 million addicted Americans and breaking the cycle of drugs and crime that has caused a massive increase in the number of people incarcerated. We need prevention programs, treatment and alternatives to incarceration for nonviolent drug offenders. Drug legalization is not a viable policy alternative because excusing harmful practices only encourages them.

At best, harm reduction is a half-way measure, a half-hearted approach that would accept defeat. Increasing help is better than decreasing harm. The "1998 National Drug Control Strategy"—a publication of the Office of National Drug Control Policy that presents a balanced mix of prevention, treatment, stiff law enforcement, interdiction and international cooperation—is a blueprint for reducing drug abuse and its consequences by half over the coming decade. With science as our guide and grass-roots organizations at the forefront, we will succeed in controlling this problem.

Pretending that harmful activity will be reduced if we condone it under the law is foolhardy and irresponsible.

The War on Drugs Must Be Continued

by Gustavo Gonzales-Baez

About the author: *Gustavo Gonzales-Baez is political affairs adviser to the Embassy of Mexico in Washington, D.C.*

The production, trafficking, and consumption of illegal drugs is one of the most serious problems faced by humankind today, both in terms of the damage done to our societies and the breakdown of government institutions. This disastrous double outcome represents a serious public-health challenge, and a threat to national security.

Both government and society are the victims of this terrible and corrupting scourge that kills and destroys. Transnational organized crime stops at nothing to control all the elements of this deadly business—from the harvesting of the drug in Asia and Latin America, to its retail sale in cities and schools in the consuming countries and the inevitable money laundering of drug profits.

The international community has slowly come to the view that this is a worldwide problem, and that to combat it requires global strategies with the participation and shared responsibility of all countries, without distinctions of hemispheres.

However, the task of reaching regional and multilateral consensus and agreements has not been an easy one. Precious time is lost due to mistrust and the inability to quickly reach accords at international forums. This slowness to react works against us, since criminal activity moves at a rapid pace within our countries, using consumption to weaken government structures. Moreover, organized crime is amazingly effective at applying the latest technology in weapons and communications equipment to its own ends, while in poor countries—who cannot respond in a like manner—drug trafficking proliferates with impunity.

An Affront to Modern States

In combating organized crime, it is not sufficient for a country to be democratically and economically strong, because organized crime has no trouble finding—or buying—protection and accomplices within the bureaucracy, police corps and the business sector. Consequently, each government must organize its law-enforcement capabilities against crime based on sound legislation as the essential legal element for effective prosecution. And it is necessary to have honest, well-paid, and properly trained police forces and prosecutors, for they are the implementing arm of justice.

But that is not all. The final objective of a well-guided justice system is to imprison drug traffickers with long sentences and seize their assets. All these elements provide the basic framework of a criminal justice system working in the right direction.

However distressing the existence of organized crime is to the international community, there are no magic solutions to eradicate it. Each country must define its national strategy based on its own priorities and the principles it has decided to observe in conjunction with other nations. A country's drug-combating program must be defined within its borders and not imposed from abroad. Any nation's attempt at meddling in another nation's affairs is bound to result in isolation and/or confrontation. The same goes for the practice of certifying a country's performance in combating drug traffic, particularly when the nation passing judgment has not herself been successful on any of the various drug fronts.

Mexico's Effort

The overcoming of the illegal-drug problem—and the wake of crime and insecurity it leaves behind—is a complex and arduous task rife with successes and setbacks. In Mexico, government and society are determined to work to the extent of their ability and talent in combating crime and impunity in drug trafficking. However, the huge wealth of the drug traffickers undermines and corrupts our police forces and Mexican prosecutors are not always sufficiently trained to conduct the necessary investigations. The Mexican judicial branch does not always act as it should to send these criminals behind bars for a long period of time.

And yet, Mexico has made great strides, which have received international recognition:

- No country in the world eradicates a greater number of illegal-drug fields than Mexico. Thirty thousand hectares are destroyed annually, with the help of 20,000 Mexican soldiers.

> *"The production, trafficking, and consumption of illegal drugs is one of the most serious problems faced by humankind today."*

- The measures taken by Mexico to combat money laundering are showing results in record time.
- A new Mexican federal law for combating organized crime introduces forms of criminal investigation that were unknown in Mexico in 1992 and

provides more tools for dismantling the major drug-trafficking cartels. Mexico's most recent successes in this area include the arrest of an entire drug-trafficking band, the dismantling of three criminal organizations involved in kidnapping, and also the dismantling of the Amezcua Contreras brothers' cartel.

- Mexico's interception efforts on its Southern border are proof of its earnest desire to stop the flow of drugs from South American countries to the U.S. market.
- Programs are being implemented to replace federal law-enforcement personnel through the use of several background checks and screening methods, including lie-detector tests. Measures have also been taken at the Police Training Institute to prepare police forces to withstand any attempts at corruption.

Respectful Relations and Cooperation

Mexico and the United States share an over two-thousand mile border. A total of 254 million persons, 75 million cars, and 3 million freight trucks cross the border annually, through 39 entry points—which represents impressive transborder activity. This provides many opportunities for legitimate trade between the two countries, but it also means that, year after year, large volumes of drugs are smuggled into the United States in response to the great demand for drugs.

> *"The final objective of a well-guided justice system is to imprison drug traffickers with long sentences and seize their assets."*

There have been problems in terms of our respective political approaches to combating illegal drugs and drug-related crime. Strategies that mistakenly placed greater emphasis on reducing the supply of drugs, and prejudiced attitudes seeking to blame others for the U.S. drug problem, led to confrontation between the two countries. Meanwhile, organized crime gained ground on the streets and in our schools and households, both in Mexico and the United States.

For many years we have engaged in mutual recriminations, and our timid attempts at cooperation have been lost in an atmosphere of mistrust and suspicion. And such attitudes have not completely disappeared, spurred on by the mass media.

A Breath of Fresh Air When All Seemed Lost

Fortunately, when all sensible arguments for coordinating forces seemed to be ignored, our countries were able to create a mechanism for binational cooperation and action between the two governments. This led to a joint threat assessment, followed by an alliance and a binational strategy that provides balance and structure to our commitments on the basis of the principles of respect to the national sovereignty of each nation.

A High Level Contact Group was created in March of 1996, pursuant to a specific mandate by presidents Ernesto Zedillo and Bill Clinton. The group provides an official framework and has led to greater mutual respect and a more structured and consistent effort on the part of both countries to comply with the commitments made in the binational strategy against drugs. The strategy covers all aspects of the drug problem, through expert groups on: demand reduction, drug interception, money laundering, drug eradication, interdiction, chemical precursors and firearms trafficking.

> *"Mexico's interception efforts on its Southern border are proof of its earnest desire to stop the flow of drugs."*

In order for this bilateral effort to be lasting and have positive results, we must work within the framework of the strategy and review our progress and setbacks with a critical but respectful attitude. We must make whatever changes are necessary and continue fighting without respite to preserve the health of our young people and our societies as a whole. There is no room for complacency and misplaced pride in this social and political task—it is important to remain objective.

An Ongoing Struggle

Mexico, the United States and the international community are aware that this is an ongoing struggle. Illegal drugs continue to be harvested, no matter how many fields we destroy. New drug cartels are formed as fast as we dismantle them, corruption undermines our police forces as inexorably as moisture destroys walls, and drug consumption figures don't come down, notwithstanding multimillion dollar budgets and investments in advertising campaigns to deter drug addiction.

The future does not look bright, but doing nothing would be our greatest failure. If we let down our guard, our young people will suffer. They will feel the full force of the drug threat, and our national security and public health will be at the mercy of organized crime.

Mexico and the United States have before them a challenge of international proportions and must continue to act in a coordinated manner, bilaterally and multilaterally, while observing their respective laws and sovereignty. And we must face other threats within our borders, such as: corruption, vested interests, pressures for drug legalization and social indifference.

Our Legacy

Sadly, it is to be expected that thousands of children and young people will continue to die due to drugs, and billions of dollars will have to be spent before we can begin to see the fruits of our work. Moreover, there will likely be more friction between our countries on the drug issue, before the binational strategy is able to partially meet its goals. This is due, in part, to our diverging national and interagency interests. However, there is nothing else we can do but continue waging this war without quarter, with all the human and financial resources at our disposal and with political determination.

Fighting against the scourge of drugs will be our legacy to future generations. We cannot foresee whether we will be successful or not, but it would be cowardly to not even try.

Organizations to Contact

The editors have compiled the following list of organizations concerned with the issues debated in this book. The descriptions are derived from materials provided by the organizations. All have publications or information available for interested readers. The list was compiled on the date of publication of the present volume; the information provided here may change. Be aware that many organizations take several weeks or longer to respond to inquiries, so allow as much time as possible.

Canadian Centre on Substance Abuse (CCSA)
75 Albert St., Suite 300, Ottawa, ON K1P 5E7 Canada
(613) 235-4048 • fax: (613) 235-8101
e-mail: info@ccsa.ca • website: www.ccsa.ca

Established in 1988 by an act of the Parliament, the CCSA works to minimize the harm associated with the use of alcohol, tobacco, and other drugs by sponsoring public debates on this issue. It disseminates information on the nature, extent, and consequences of substance abuse and supports organizations involved in substance abuse treatment, prevention, and educational programming. The center publishes the newsletter *Action News* six times a year.

Canadian Foundation for Drug Policy (CFDP)
70 MacDonald St., Ottawa, ON K2P 1H6 Canada
(613) 236-1027 • fax: (613) 238-2891
e-mail: eoscapel@fox.nstn.ca • website: www.cfdp.ca

Founded by several of Canada's leading drug policy specialists, the CFDP examines the objectives and consequences of Canada's drug laws and policies. When necessary, the foundation recommends alternatives that it believes would make Canada's drug policies more effective and humane. The CFDP disseminates educational materials and maintains a website.

Cato Institute
1000 Massachusetts Ave. NW, Washington, DC 20001-5403
(202) 842-0200 • fax: (202) 842-3490
e-mail: cato@cato.org • website: www.cato.org

The institute, a libertarian public policy research foundation, is dedicated to limiting the control of government and to protecting individual liberty. Cato, which strongly favors drug legalization, publishes the *Cato Journal* three times a year and the bimonthly *Cato Policy Report*.

Drug Enforcement Administration (DEA)
Information Services Section (CPI)
2401 Jefferson Davis Hwy., Arlington, VA 22301
website: www.usdoj.gov/dea

The DEA is the federal agency charged with enforcing the nation's drug laws. The agency concentrates on stopping the smuggling and distribution of narcotics in the United States and abroad. It publishes the *Drug Enforcement Magazine* three times a year.

Heritage Foundation

214 Massachusetts Ave. NE, Washington, DC 20008-2302
(202) 546-4400 • fax: (202) 546-8328
e-mail: info@heritage.org • website: www.heritage.org

The Heritage Foundation is a conservative public policy research institute that opposes the legalization of drugs and advocates strengthening law enforcement to stop drug abuse. It publishes position papers on a broad range of topics, including drug issues. The foundation's regular publications include the monthly *Policy Review,* the Backgrounder series of occasional papers, and the Heritage Lecture series.

Institute for a Drug-Free Workplace

1225 I St. NW, Suite 1000, Washington, DC 20005-3914
(202) 842-7400 • fax: (202) 842-0022
website: www.drugfreeworkplace.org

The institute is dedicated to preserving the rights of employers and employees in substance-abuse prevention programs and to positively influencing the national debate on these issues. It publishes the *Guide to Dangerous Drugs,* the pamphlets *What Every Employee Should Know About Drug Abuse: Answers to 20 Good Questions* and *Does Drug Testing Work?* as well as several fact sheets.

Libertarian Party

2600 Pennsylvania Ave. NW, Suite 100, Washington, DC 20037
(202) 333-0008 • fax: (202) 333-0072
e-mail: hq@lp.org • website: www.lp.org

The Libertarian Party is a political party aiming to protect individual rights and liberties. It advocates the repeal of all laws prohibiting the production, sale, possession, or use of drugs. The party believes law enforcement should focus on preventing violent crimes against persons and property rather than on prosecuting people who use drugs. It publishes the bimonthly *Libertarian Party News* and periodic *Issues Papers* and distributes a compilation of articles supporting drug legalization.

The Lindesmith Center-Drug Policy Foundation (TCL-DPF)

4455 Connecticut Ave. NW, Suite B-500, Washington, DC 20008-2328
(202) 537-5005 • fax: (202) 537-3007
e-mail: information@drugpolicy.org • website: www.lindesmith.org

The Lindesmith Center and Drug Policy Foundation, two major drug policy organizations, merged on July 1, 2000, and became TLC-DPF. TLC-DPF seeks to educate Americans and others about alternatives to current drug policies on issues ranging from marijuana and adolescent drug use to illicit drug addiction, the spread of infectious diseases, policing drug markets, and alternatives to incarceration. It addresses issues of drug policy reform through a variety of projects, including the International Harm Reduction Development (IHRD), a response to increased drug use and HIV transmissions in eastern Europe. The center also publishes fact sheets on topics such as needle and syringe availability, drug prohibition and the U.S. prison system, and drug education.

Narcotics Anonymous (NA)

World Services Office
PO Box 9999,Van Nuys, CA 91409
(818) 773-9999 • fax: (818) 700-0700

Narcotics Anonymous, comprising more than eighteen thousand groups worldwide, is an organization of recovering drug addicts who meet regularly to help each other abstain from drugs. It publishes the monthly *NA Way Magazine* and annual conference reports.

National Center on Addiction and Substance Abuse at Columbia University (CASA)

633 3rd Ave., 19th Floor, New York, NY 10017-6706
(212) 841-5200
website: www.casacolumbia.org

CASA is a private, nonprofit organization that works to educate the public about the hazards of chemical dependency. The organization supports treatment as the best way to reduce chemical dependency. It produces publications describing the harmful effects of alcohol and drug addiction and effective ways to address the problem of substance abuse. Its recent reports include the "National Survey of American Attitudes on Substance Abuse VI: Teens."

National Institute on Drug Abuse (NIDA)

U.S. Department of Health and Human Services
6001 Executive Blvd., Room 5213, Bethesda, MD 20892
(301) 443-1124
e-mail: information@lists.nida.hih.gov • website: www.nida.nih.gov

NIDA supports and conducts research on drug abuse—including the yearly *Monitoring the Future Survey*—in order to improve addiction prevention, treatment, and policy efforts. It publishes the bimonthly *NIDA Notes* newsletter, the periodic *NIDA Fact Sheets*, and a catalog of research reports and public education materials such as *Marijuana: Facts for Teens.*

National Organization for the Reform of Marijuana Laws (NORML)

1001 Connecticut Ave. NW, Suite 710, Washington, DC 20036
(202) 483-5500 • fax: (202) 483-0057
e-mail: norml@norml.org • website: www.norml.org

NORML fights to legalize marijuana and to help those who have been convicted and sentenced for possessing or selling marijuana. The organization publishes an on-line newsletter, reports, and books including *Marihuana: The Forbidden Medicine* and *Marijuana Myths, Marijuana Facts.*

Office of National Drug Control Policy (ONDCP)

Drug Policy Information Clearinghouse
PO Box 6000, Rockville, MD 20849-6000
(800) 666-3332 • fax: (301) 519-5212
e-mail: ondcp@ncjrs.org • website: www.whitehousedrugpolicy.gov

The Office of National Drug Control Policy is responsible for formulating the government's national drug strategy and the president's antidrug policy as well as coordinating the federal agencies responsible for stopping drug trafficking. Its recent reports include "Estimation of Heroin Availability" and "Pulse Check: Midyear 2000."

RAND Corporation

1700 Main St., PO Box 2138, Santa Monica, CA 90407-2138
(310) 393-0411, ext. 4818
e-mail: feedback@rand.org • website: www.rand.org

The RAND Corporation is a research institution that seeks to improve public policy through research and analysis. RAND's Drug Policy Research Center publishes information on the costs, prevention, and treatment of alcohol and drug abuse as well as on trends in drug-law enforcement. Its extensive list of publications includes the book *Colombian Labyrinth: The Synergy of Drugs and Insurgency and Its Implications for Regional Stability.*

Reason Foundation
3451 S. Sepulveda Blvd., Suite 400, Los Angeles, CA 90034
(310) 391-2245 • fax: (310) 391-4395
e-mail: gpassantino@reason.org • website: www.reason.org

This public policy organization researches contemporary social and political problems and promotes libertarian philosophy and free-market principles. It publishes the monthly *Reason* magazine, which contains articles and editorials critical of the war on drugs and smoking regulation.

Substance Abuse and Mental Health Services Administration (SAMHSA)
5600 Fishers Ln., Rockville, MD 20857
e-mail: info@samhsa.gov • website: www.samhsa.gov

SAMHSA is a federal agency aimed at improving the quality and availability of prevention, treatment, and rehabilitative services in order to reduce illness, death, disability, and cost to society resulting from drug abuse and mental illnesses. It publishes the newsletter *SAMHSA News* and provides resources for drug abuse information and statistics.

Bibliography

Books

Rachel Green Baldino — *Welcome to Methadonia: A Social Worker's Candid Account of Life in a Methadone Clinic.* Harrisburg, PA: White Hat Communications, 2001.

Patrick L. Clawson and Rensselaer W. Lee III — *The Andean Cocaine Industry.* New York: St. Martin's Press, 1998.

Sean Connolly — *Amphetamines (Just the Facts).* Crystal Lake, IL: Heinemann Library, 2000.

Ross Coomber, ed. — *The Control of Drugs and Drug Users: Reason or Reaction?* Amsterdam: Harwood Academic, 1998.

Robert L. Dupont and Betty Ford — *The Selfish Brain: Learning from Addiction.* Washington, DC: Hazelden Information Education, 2000.

Patricia G. Erickson et al. — *Harm Reduction: A New Direction for Drug Policies and Programs.* Toronto: University of Toronto Press, 1997.

James P. Gray — *Why Our Drug Laws Have Failed and What We Can Do About It: A Judicial Indictment on the War on Drugs.* Philadelphia: Temple University Press, 2001.

Glen Hanson, Peter Venturelli, and Annette E. Fleckenstein, eds. — *Drugs and Society.* Boston: Jones and Bartlett, 2001.

Jim Hogshire — *Pills a Go Go: Fiendish Investigation into Pill Marketing, Art, History, and Consumption.* Los Angeles: Feral House, 1999.

Kent Holtorf and Angie Vandael — *Ur-Ine Trouble: How Drug Users Are Passing and Nonusers Are Failing.* Scottsdale, AZ: Vandalay Press, 1998.

Raymond M. Jamiolkoski — *Drugs and Domestic Violence.* Washington, DC: Hazelden Information Education, 1997.

David C. Jordan — *Drug Politics: Dirty Money and Democracies.* Norman: University of Oklahoma Press, 1999.

Cynthia Kuhn et al. — *Buzzed: The Straight Facts About the Most Used Drugs from Alcohol to Ecstasy.* New York: W.W. Norton, 1998.

Bibliography

David M. MacDowell and Henry I. Spitz — *Substance Abuse: From Principles to Practice*. Philadelphia: Brunner/Mazel, 1999.

Geoffrey Pearson, ed. — *Drugs and the End of the Century*. Oxford: University of Oxford Press, 1999.

Cheryl Pellerin — *Trips: How Hallucinogens Work in Your Brain*. New York: Seven Stories Press, 1998.

Craig Reinarman and Harry Gene Levine, eds. — *Crack in America: Demon Drugs and Social Justice*. Berkeley: University of California Press, 1997.

Marc Allen Schuckit — *Educating Yourself About Drugs and Alcohol: A People's Primer*. New York: Plenum Trade, 1998.

Lonny Shavelson — *Hooked: Five Addicts Challenge Our Misguided Rehab System*. New York: New Press, 2001.

Nigel South, ed. — *Drugs, Controls, and Everyday Life*. Thousand Oaks, CA: Sage Publications, 1999.

Sally J. Stevens and Harry K. Wexler, eds. — *Women and Substance Abuse: Gender Transparency*. New York: Haworth Press, 1998.

Samuel Walker — *Sense and Nonsense About Crime and Drugs: A Policy Guide*. Belmont, CA: Wadsworth, 2000.

Andrew Weil and Winifred Rosen — *From Chocolate to Morphine: Everything You Need to Know About Mind-Altering Drugs*. Boston: Houghton-Mifflin, 1998.

Brett Alan Weinberg and Bonnie K. Bealer — *The World of Caffeine: The Science and Culture of the World's Most Popular Drug*. New York: Routledge, 2001.

Lynn Zimmer and John P. Morgan — *Marijuana Myths, Marijuana Facts: A Review of the Scientific Evidence*. New York: Lindesmith Center, 1997.

Periodicals

American Academy of Pediatrics — "Marijuana: A Growing Concern for Parents," *American Academy of Pediatrics*, October 1999.

Joseph A. Califano Jr. — "It's All in the Family," *America*, January 15, 2000.

John Cloud — "Recreational Pharmaceuticals," *Time*, January 6, 2001.

James L. Curtis — "Clean but Not Safe," *New York Times*, April 22, 1998.

Christopher John Farley — "Rave New World," *Time*, June 5, 2000.

Daniel Hill — "Drug Money," *Brandweek*, April 27, 1998.

Molly Ivins — "Drug Policy Has Created the World's Largest Penal System," *Liberal Opinion*, March 15, 1999.

Sharon Lerner — "Legal Needles," *Village Voice*, May 23, 2000.

Joseph D. McNamara — "The War America Lost," *Hoover Digest*, 2000.

Eric Meers — "Short Circuit," *Advocate*, December 22, 1998.

Drug Abuse

Mike Mitka	"Abuse of Prescription Drugs: Is a Patient Ailing or Addicted?" *Journal of American Medical Association*, March 2000.
Betty Pisik	"Online Traffickers Fuel Pill Popping Culture," *Insight*, April 6, 2001.
David Oliver Relin	"Drug E-mergency," *Teen People*, March 2001.
Bill Ritter	"Fighting the Real War on Drugs," *World & I*, February 2000.
Ryan H. Sager	"Teach Them Well: Drug Talk That Fails," *National Review,* May 1, 2000.
Sally L. Satel	"Do Drug Courts Really Work?" *City Journal*, Summer 1998.
Robert Scheer	"Smugglers' Youth Ends at Border," *Los Angeles Times*, September 9, 2000.
Phyllis Schlafly	"Better Research on Drugs Needed," *Conservative Chronicle*, April 18, 2001.
Stephanie Stapleton	"Is Your Patient (or Child) Abusing Inhalants?" *American Medical News*, April 9, 2001.
Jennifer Steinhauer	"Club Owners Become Focus of Effort to Combat Drug Abuse," *New York Times*, April 28, 2001.
Thomas Szasz	"Progress in Pain Relief," *Ideas on Liberty*, September 2000.

Index

Drug Abuse

Galbraith, John Kenneth, 43
Gamma 10, 53–54
Gardner, Dan, 130
Georgia Home Boy, 53–54
Germany, 134
GHB (gamma-hydroxybutyrate), 53–54, 55
Gibbs, Landon, 67
Glasglow, Scotland, 15
Goldstein, Avram, 153–54
Gonzales-Baez, Gustavo, 155
Gook, 53–54
Great Britain, 145
green. See ketamine
Grevious Bodily Harm, 53–54
G-riffick, 53–54
Griffith, Melanie, 66
GWM, 52

hallucinogens
  development of tolerance to, 63
  effects of, 60–62, 63–64
  synthetic, 61–62
  unmask pre-existing psychological
    problems, 63
  unpredictability of, 62
  use of, 61
  varieties of, 61–62
  see also ketamine; LSD
harm reduction approach
  described, 14–15, 138
  does not increase drug use, 138
  is halfhearted measure, 154
  is ineffective, 16
  legalization is true intent of, 152
  in Netherlands, 15, 137
  and offenders, 14
  theory of, 152
  view drug abuse as spanning spectrum,
    14, 16
  see also methadone; needle-exchange
    programs
Harrison Act, 147
Hatch, Orrin G., 127
hemp. See marijuana
hepatitis B, 15, 96
hepatitis C, 56, 57, 59, 84
Herbal Bliss, 52
Herbal X, 52
heroin
  arrests from sale of, 123
  deaths from, 46, 58, 74, 118
  diseases from, 56, 57, 59, 84
  in England, 145
  euphoric rush of, 86
  forms of, 57

marketing of, 142
nasal administration of, 47
in Netherlands, 134, 138
and teenagers, 46
use of, 38, 47, 71, 132
  age at, 74
  and functionality, 31
  increase in, 42, 57, 84
  prior to prohibition, 132
and Vietnam War veterans, 22
withdrawal symptoms of, 21
  see also methadone
Hitt, R. Scott, 95
HIV, 139
  and heroin, 84
  and needle-exchange programs
    in Canada, 114
    reduce risk of, 15
    con, 15–16
  transmission of, 96–97, 98, 114
    and methadone maintenance, 86
    needle-exchange programs reduce, 95,
      96, 98
Hoffman, Albert, 61
Hoffman-La Roche, 52
Hogen, Robin, 77–78
Holland. See Netherlands

ice. See methamphetamine
immune system, 150
immunization, 29
imprisonment. See criminal justice system
India, 131
inhalants, 48, 71
Institute of Medicine (IOM), 28, 32, 35
Issues in Science and Technology
  (magazine), 152
Italy, 134

jimsonweed, 60, 61
Johnson, Gary E., 117
Johnston, Lloyd D., 89
Jones, David, 77
Joranson, David E., 69
Justice Policy Institute, 133

Kalb, Claudia, 65
Ketaject, 54
Ketalar, 54
ketamine, 54, 60–61, 62
Kit Kat. See ketamine
Klam, Michael, 54
Kleber, Herbert, 142
Kleiman, Mark, 149
Knowledge-Attitude-Behavior (K-A-B)

170